MW01168716

WHAT

*IN THE BOSOM OF ABRAHAM*

Amy's writing always leads me to delight and
wonder. The old familiar stories of my Jewish
roots are suddenly imbued with freshness and
intrigue.

—Hanna Miley,
Messianic Jewish author

Following Amy Cogdell's private conversation
with the Lord, we are drawn into His presence,
coming under His blessing. Abraham appears
in an all-new light, becoming our teacher,
counselor, and friend. You will discover, even
in these first chapters of the Bible, something
of the mysteries of Calvary. And we learn to
listen to the voice of the Beloved of our soul.
Like the bride from the Song of Solomon, we
are longing to respond to His love with an
undivided heart.

—Sister Joela Krüger,
Evangelical Sisters of Mary

Rather than starting with the common—but
incorrect—assumption that the Gentile
Christian church has superseded the people of
Israel in God's global plan, Amy Cogdell

begins by taking seriously Paul's description of herself as "grafted in" to the original olive tree—the Jews. From that starting point, she embarks on a surprising exploration of her identity as a daughter of the father of the faith.

—Deacon Johannes Fichtenbauer,
European Network of Communities

Amy Cogdell's writings usher the reader in beautiful ways into God's presence. She imparts uncommon insights with gentleness and sensitivity, making them easily accessible. *In the Bosom of Abraham* will be a spiritual treasure for many.

—George Miley,
Cofounder, Antioch Network

# IN THE
# BOSOM
## *of*
# ABRAHAM

REFLECTIONS OF A GENTILE ON THE
FATHERHOOD OF ABRAHAM AND HIS
GOD

Amy M Cogdell

Cogdell Creative

In the Bosom of Abraham: Reflections of a Gentile on the Fatherhood of Abraham and His God

Published by Cogdell Creative, cogdellcreative.space
Printed in the United States of America.

Cover Design: Pradeep Premalal
Publishing Consultant: Inksnatcher
Author Photo: Abigail Cogdell

ISBN 978-1-960196-08-8 – Paperback

ISBN 978-1-960196-07-1 – eBook

*For Caroline, a friend of God who has shown me*

*how to walk in His ways.*

*So it was that the beggar died, and was carried by*

*the angels to Abraham's bosom.*

–Luke 16:22

# CONTENTS

# Acknowledgments

While the musings contained in the following pages are not taken straight from my journal, most of them began as private prayers and meditations. It is a fearful step to invite others into such a personal space. Thus, I am grateful for the friends who read early drafts of this book with such care. I am thinking of Caroline, Marianna, Rose and her father, and my husband Thomas. Their encouragement kept me writing, and their feedback helped corral my wonderings within the bounds of sound Christian doctrine.

I am especially thankful for Rabbi Mark Kinzer, Ph.D., who not only read the manuscript but also challenged some of my conceptions of faith. Several times, Mark's comments sent me back to prayer, Scripture, and contemplation. I am richer for his input, and I trust the work is more robust.

Blessings upon Deb and Sid Davila, who opened their Yeshiva Retreat as a place for me to write. And also upon Sandi Pedrotti, whose deep and thoughtful love for the God of Abraham, Isaac, and Jacob has shaped my own heart and mind.

Finally, many thanks to Bob Fullilove, my copyeditor, who tracked down the sources of all the Bible quotes that I mixed and matched in various translations. I sent him a messy, free-flowing manuscript and he returned a tidy, proper book. It was a labor of love for which I am duly grateful.

# FOREWORD

*By Rabbi Mark Kinzer, Ph.D.*

What sort of book is this that now rests in your hands, or scrolls on your screen?

A biblical meditation on a portion of Scripture? Yes, but of a peculiar sort. Most biblical meditations address the reader directly, and offer their insights on the text as a guide to its riches. In these pages we are invited instead to listen in on thoughts and questions about the story of Abraham, directed not to us but to the God of Abraham. The immediate audience for these meditations is the One who is a character in that story, the inspirer of the text that recounts the story, and the Father of the Messiah who will bring the story to completion. It is this One who through the Messiah has graciously included Amy Cogdell (and presumably her readers) in the family of Abraham's descendants.

Does this mean that we are reading an extended prayer? Yes, but a prayer of an unusual sort. Like the theological writings of Augustine or Anselm that are offered in the form and posture of prayer, Cogdell practices exegesis in the presence of God. She asks questions about the story of Abraham and offers possible answers to them, as one who is not really addressing the questions to herself or to the text, but instead to the One who alone can truly answer them.

Is this, then, exclusively a prayerful meditation on the biblical story? It is, in fact, more than that. Like Augustine's *Confessions*, this short book also contains Cogdell's reflection on her own life, which she ponders in relation to what the Bible says about Abraham. She marvels at the fact that she herself has been grafted to the covenant God makes with Abraham. Because of that ingrafting, Abraham is now her father, and she can locate and understand her own story as previewed and interpreted by his.

But, as one whose relationship to Abraham has been established by his messianic seed, she also interprets the story of Abraham in light of the story of Jesus. This rightly generates awe at the true weight borne by Abraham's faith, a weight whose magnitude Abraham could only sense dimly. Certainly, Abraham was told that his many descendants would be the recipients and conveyors of abundant blessing. But he could not possibly envision that his response to the divine call and promise would result in the healing and divinization of the cosmos. And perhaps that measure of ignorance was itself a divine gift.

By publishing these meditative expository prayers, Cogdell invites us to share her wonder, and to connect to Abraham and Abraham's God, in the same way that she has. She does not treat Abraham as a wooden figure from an ancient text who can teach us moral or spiritual lessons, but as a man in full who has become the father of all who are joined to the God of Israel. The drama of his life has become the drama of her life, and both of their lives are viewed in relation to the drama of the life of the Messiah.

Like Abraham, Amy Cogdell is a person of faith and vision, a physical and spiritual parent whose relationship with God has been a blessing to many. I am grateful for the opportunity to overhear some of what goes on in her prayerful meditation on Scripture. Whatever else this special little book might be, I am sure that it is this: a personal gift to each of us, inviting us to embark or continue the journey of faith that began with Abraham and reached its consummation in the death and resurrection of his messianic seed.

# 1

# THE VOICE

*Now the Lord had said to Abram:*
*"Get out of your country,*
*From your family*
*And from your father's house,*
*To a land that I will show you.*
*I will make you a great nation;*
*I will bless you*
*And make your name great;*
*And you shall be a blessing.*
*I will bless those who bless you,*
*And I will curse him who curses you;*
*And in you all the families of the earth shall be*
*blessed."*
*—Genesis 12:1–3*

A VOICE. THAT WAS ALL.

Except for the stars, of course, and the mountains. Creation was Your witness, but there were no books. Or rules. Or religion.

Legends, yes, of a distant past in which God walked with men. Sacrifice, perhaps, made to powers unseen. But there were no examples, no teachers for the man You chose. It had to be that way in the beginning. The start of salvation history served as a foretaste of its end when we will have no need of teachers. Someday "the earth will be filled with the knowledge of the glory of the Lord, as the waters cover the sea" (Hab. 2:14).

I wonder what You saw in Abram that moved You so deeply? You spoke to him in human words, appointing him as the hinge on which the Gate of Salvation would swing. What led You to seal him with such friendship? Was it something similar to what you recognized in Mary? Was it awe? humility? longing? How do You choose those to whom You open Your thoughts?

And what was it like for Abram to hear Your voice that day? How did it feel to know that the One who called the universe into being was calling to him? How did he dare to believe that a voice from heaven had descended upon a middle-aged man in Haran?

Your voice must have been electrifying, exhilarating, consoling, and petrifying all at once. Your word is power. It transcends human imagination. When we hear it, our souls are shaken. Or rather, they are plowed, laid bare, and tested.

Those who hear You must respond. We must choose to believe or disbelieve. We will either follow You, or we will turn to our own way. And this truth sets my head spinning—You are moved when we believe! You rejoice in those who respond in faith. You give them a seed that takes root in the soul, growing, branching out, sweeping new generations into its promise until it reaches a fruition "exceedingly abundantly above all that we ask or think" (Eph. 3:20).

Scripture tells us that You spoke to Abram several times before You released the Seed—the covenant that marked the man who would father Your own family tree. You are kind to Your prophets that way, introducing Yourself slowly, mindful that we humans are dust. You spoke to Moses in a burning bush before coming in a pillar of fire. You fed Elijah with ravens before lifting him to heaven in a whirlwind. You showed Jeremiah a watching tree before revealing the pot of destruction.

You sent an angel to prepare Mary before You overshadowed her Yourself.

3

With Abram, I suspect You began even more slowly, for You were doing a new thing upon the earth. Never before had You bound Yourself to one man's descendants. Never before had You made such an extravagant promise. Never before had You opened Your heart so fully to a human.

Abraham knew You as Creator and Ruler of the heavens. Isaac, in turn, would know You as the God of his father. Jacob called You the God of Abraham and Isaac. All men afterward would speak of You as the God of Abraham, Isaac, and Jacob.

Why should you, the Almighty, choose to be known by the names of Your friends? Such humility is an expression of a Father's love. Fatherhood is the joy from which Your action springs. It is the end for which the world was made. It is the mystery into which You called Abram and his descendants.

I like to imagine You sitting in heaven studying Abraham on earth, just as I watched my own son in his youth, attentive to those things that would captivate his imagination. Perhaps Abraham's soul thrilled at the beauty of Your creation, and he responded by singing Your praise. Maybe he was a philosopher wondering about the source of life. Scripture indicates that Abraham was a man who loved justice and showed mercy to his neighbors.

Whatever the connection, You loved the man who would become Your friend. You worked patiently to make Yourself known to him, for on the day he heard Your voice, his heart was ready to run.

I find it interesting that the first iteration of the promise made no mention of a son. You spoke of a nation, and a name, and a blessing for every family of the earth. You wrote the promise large with the end in sight; but You did not tell the path of its fulfillment. You did not warn Abraham of his testing. Nor did You reveal Your own interest in this plan. Abram had no clue Your greatest desire was wrapped into his promise. That was a mystery held for a later time. You restrained Yourself when You spoke to Abram, both for his sake and for ours; and yet Your fatherly love must have burned in Your voice, igniting the heart of Your friend.

The wonder of that encounter stretched Abram's yearning in ways hard for mortals to bear. A name, a nation, and the blessing of the whole world—who would dare to dream of such a blessing? The fulfillment of the promise lay as far out of Abram's grasp as bearing God's Son would lay beyond Mary's. Yet humility enabled them both to believe.

Abram packed his bags quickly and departed Haran with his wife and nephew.

Moving was the only thanks he had to offer, and the best hope of hearing Your voice again. I strongly suspect that the intoxication of Your presence lured Abraham more than the promise of blessing.

I wonder how Abraham mulled that fateful decision in the decades of his waiting? How often did he doubt his calling? How deeply did Sarah question her husband's sanity? Whatever hopes Abraham held for children, for the land, and for a nation to be birthed from his loins must have grown dimmer year after year. Yet the promise remained certain for it was vouchsafed in Your own heart.

You have been unfolding the mystery of Abram's election ever since You called out to him from heaven. Your voice has called to prophets, generation after generation, revealing ever new dimensions of the promise. How thankful I am for the friends You have found on earth! How I love to read their stories! Women and men who bear the strain of a hope anchored in heaven are a gift in this dark world. Their faith calls forth my own. Their witness assures me that You speak and that I can trust in Your voice. But among all the prophets, Abraham and Mary stand apart, for to them You entrusted Your Seed. They are the beginning and end points of the covenant through which You bind Yourself to men.

Even Yeshua, Your Only Begotten, calls them father and mother.

I am learning from You, humble Father, how to honor my father Abraham. I am growing in awe of him as I contemplate the immensity of the blessing You conferred upon him. And as I contemplate Your friendship with men, I am coming to love You more.

Bold as it sounds, I cannot help but imagine You saw me on the day You told Abraham to count the stars. I cannot help but think You are studying me now, even as I study my spiritual father. I believe such study pleases you. Furthermore, I dare to hope that Abraham knows me, or at least he will on the day I am carried to his bosom. We are gifts to one another—Abraham and I—the way a father and daughter should be. This is the joy, my Father, that You have ordained.

# 2

# THE PROMISE

*"It is too small a thing that You should be My Servant*
*To raise up the tribes of Jacob,*
*And to restore the preserved ones of Israel;*
*I will also give You as a light to the Gentiles,*
*That You should be My salvation to the ends of the*
*earth."*
*—Isaiah 49:6*

*Jesus answered, "Your father Abraham rejoiced to see*
*My day, and he saw it and was glad."*
*Then the Jews said to Him, "You are not yet fifty years*
*old, and have You seen Abraham?"*
*Jesus said to them, "Most assuredly, I say to you,*
*before Abraham was, I AM."*
*—John 8:54–58*

YOUR PLAN PRECEDED ABRAHAM. This
is the mystery that I have failed to grasp most
of my life. The union of God with man was
planned before the dawn of time. The way of
salvation was conceived in the counsel of the
Godhead. The promise was agreed upon by
Three Holy Witnesses—Father, Son, and Spirit.
"The Lamb [was] slain from the foundation of
the world" (Rev. 13:8). For this reason,
Abraham's blessing is unshakable. It is why
Paul could write with confidence that You, my
Lord, "preached the gospel to Abraham
beforehand" (Gal. 3:8).

Abraham was the first to hear the gospel,
and the first to be saved by faith. He also was
the first to receive the physical seed that would
bear its fruit in the Incarnation. Thus,
Abraham is the father of both Jew and Gentile.
This mystery of salvation has always been a
double mystery—conceived in heaven yet
enacted on earth. Sealed in eternity but
unveiled in time. Saving both flesh and spirit.
Most astoundingly, to my mind at least, the
promise carries hope for both God and man.
Your desire for our salvation exceeds our own,
for You see its glorious end. It was for the joy
set before Him that You sent Your Son to bear
the cross.

The Incarnation of Your Son, I believe, is a
sign for Your people on earth. Jesus is both

God and man, united in one Person. In a similar way, Your people are both Jew and Gentile, held together in Your Only Begotten. Two distinct branches receive life from One Vine. We cannot separate ourselves from one another without severing ourselves from the Vine. Any attempt to do so is an attack on the Vine itself. It is a rejection either of our Savior's love for the family of His flesh or His brethren born of faith. It is a diminishing of the mystery of the Incarnation. It is an expression of foolish, short-sighted pride.

The humility of Jesus puts the rest of us humans to shame. Your Only Begotten, though equal with You, was not ashamed to call mortals His brethren. He lived with us, ate with us, depended upon human help, bore our insults, and received our comfort. He cleaves to us still, opening the way to heaven to both Jew and Gentile. But we vie against one another to prove ourselves great. We grasp at prophecies—sometimes spiritualizing them, other times minimizing them—to claim them as our own. We disregard the incarnational, flesh-and-spirit, Jew-and-Gentile mystery of Your people. No wonder Paul urgently charges believers to "have the same attitude that Christ Jesus had" (Phil. 2:5 NLT)! When we focus on ourselves, we lose sight of the most glorious, most astounding truth about the promise—that

11

it was made for Your joy! The highest honor of any child of Abraham should be to seek the fullness of the promise for the sake of Your pleasure, just as Jesus did.

I believe it brings You joy, Father, for me to love those whom You love. Abraham is Your friend, and so I want to know him. I want to love him as You do and thus share in Your friendship. That is the hope that drives these musings of mine.

These days I often find myself longing, like Lazarus in the parable, to rest "in the bosom of Abraham." I used to think that image was a strange consolation for Jesus to put forth to His audience. Why talk about the ministrations of a Jewish patriarch when there were flashier wonders for Lazarus to enjoy? Why did Jesus not mention the streets of gold, the choirs of angels, the tree of life, and the wedding feast?

I realize, of course, that this is a parable. Abraham's role, in part, is to emphasize the gulf between heaven and Hades. But Jesus speaks of Abraham so matter-of-factly that I'm inclined to believe such introductions do indeed happen, and that they are more consoling than we can imagine. Abraham laughs in wonder as he counts each star born of his line. Each of his children, in turn, marvels at being known. Each child finds her place in Your story while resting in Abraham's arms. And You, Father, look on with a smile as the promise conceived in the heart of the Godhead expands beyond Your children's wildest dreams.

# 3

# DROUGHT

*Now there was a famine in the land, and Abram went down to Egypt to dwell there, for the famine was severe in the land.*
*—Genesis 12:10*

ONE WONDERFUL THING ABOUT
PARENTS is that they know the ways of the
world. They navigate twisting routes to school,
or to church, or even faraway cities, with
effortless ease. They have mastered the secret
arts of tying knots and filing taxes. They cause
food to appear promptly at dinner time. With
one look at the sky, they can tell when a storm
is brewing. What would children do without
their fathers and mothers?

Spiritual parents are no less important for
they know the ways of God. They are a gift
from You, our Heavenly Father, to help us on
our journeys. Spiritual fathers and mothers
have stories to tell. They have heard Your voice
in the wilderness and languished through
seasons of silence. They have seen Your hand
in battle and felt the sting of the enemy's
mockery. They have suffered the consequences
of straying off the map and have known Your
mercy for the prodigal. Their stories serve as
fuel for the faith of future generations. Not
that anyone can follow precisely in their
footsteps. You set a course that is unique for
every person whom You call. Yet the vehicle by
which we approach Your gates remains the
same: Without faith it is impossible to please
You (see Heb. 11:6).

Abraham serves the whole world as a
spiritual father. He was not the first man You

created. Nor was he the first prophet. Enoch and Noah both knew Your voice and walked in Your ways. But Abraham was the first to hear the gospel, veiled thickly in the promise (see Gal. 3:8). He was the first to hear the good news and believe. He was also the first to receive the mark of circumcision—a sign that set his seed apart. He was the first to carry the hope of a Messiah in his physical body. For this reason he is rightly counted as father both to Jews and to Gentiles who believe in the Jewish Messiah.

Because Abraham's role in salvation history would prove so pivotal, You gave him a wild and lengthy story. Your friend had much to learn about faith, and You had much to show us. His first lesson was a mystical encounter with Your voice. But mysticism was followed by action. Abraham packed his bags and hit the road to prove his faith. When he arrived in Canaan, You spoke to Your friend again, pledging the land as an inheritance to his descendants. I imagine that Abraham expected to meet You there. But then something unexpected happened. The land of Your choosing, the land You promised to Your friend, was struck with famine. Canaan became uninhabitable.

How curious. And disappointing.

I wonder if Abraham doubted Your word, Lord?

Did he wonder if he had dreamed it all?

How long did he pray for rain before packing his bags for Egypt?

Did he ask Your counsel?

Were You silent?

You do not tell us. Abraham's internal struggle remains private, like our internal battles.

Abraham fled to Egypt seeking to save his life, but he anticipated a problem. His wife Sarah was exceedingly beautiful, and Pharaoh was exceedingly powerful. Once Pharaoh saw her, Abraham reasoned, he would take Sarah for himself. The fact that she was a married woman would present no obstacle. Pharaoh was accustomed to getting his way. His servants would kill without hesitation at their ruler's command.

There is no indication in Scripture, Lord, that Abraham asked for Your counsel. Not in this matter. In fear he hatched a plan of his own, pleading with Sarah to claim she was his sister. That way, he figured, Pharaoh would take her without killing him.

I wonder how Abraham reconciled this scheme with the word of promise. Did he plan to abandon Sarah to Pharaoh and return to Canaan without her? Did he intend to stay in Egypt forever, forfeiting Your call? Or was he simply flailing in fear, incapable of considering the future?

Abraham's worry was justified. Pharaoh was smitten by Sarah's beauty. She lied as instructed, and Pharaoh took her as a bride. But before he could touch her, You intervened, striking Pharaoh's household with plagues.

My Lord, You were more jealous for the promise than Abraham could comprehend! And You loved Your friend more than he imagined. If Abraham had possessed any inkling of the favor in which he walked, he would never have feared Pharaoh. If he had understood Sarah's importance in Your plan, he would never have risked his marriage. But You knew Abraham's vision was limited. Faith grows in the darkness of human limitation. It is the "substance of things hoped for, the evidence of things not seen." (Heb. 11:1). You were building Abraham's faith, even in the failure of his lies.

Because You held the promise safely in Your hands, Pharaoh returned Sarah to her husband. The king of Egypt was rightly filled with dread of Your prophet and bade him leave. Thus Abraham was driven back to Canaan, where the land was parched and dry.

Drought often follows on the heels of revelation. That is Your design. The path of faith invariably passes through barren landscapes, for love must be tested.

Joseph walked a similar path to his great-grandfather. He was also a man favored by You. Shortly after sending him two wonderful, mystical dreams, Joseph's brothers betrayed him and sold him into slavery. Years later, Lord, You struck Canaan with famine. Joseph's brothers traveled to Egypt seeking provision, much as Abraham had done.

Perhaps the famine was Your judgment for the sin against Joseph. Perhaps the hunger was a gift. Maybe You were driving the sons to Israel to a reconciliation. Whatever Your reasons, we know that You were in control. The drought was Your tool. And the story You were writing was glorious indeed. Joseph forgave his brothers, and Abraham's family was reunited.

The sons of Israel ate well in Egypt. As they grew fat, the promise grew dim in their collective memory. They failed to meditate on its magnitude. They failed to seek Your voice. Like Esau, they despised their birthright. They first became slaves to their bellies, and then slaves to the Egyptians.

But You remained faithful to the promise, for it was written upon Your heart. You would not let go of Abraham's children. You would not choose another family for Your Only Begotten. So once again You chose a friend to Yourself. And once again You brought down plagues upon Pharaoh. But this time You worked wonders on behalf of an entire nation, signs never seen before or since. You led Israel out with a pillar of fire. You parted the Red Sea for Your people. You plundered their oppressors and adorned them in gold. You made their hearts sing in wonder and awe.

Then, as You had done with Abraham, you tested them with hunger.

Drought often follows on the heels of revelation.

My spiritual fathers and mothers have taught me that drought is not always punishment. On the contrary, the desert is where You train Your prophets. It is where Moses, Elijah, and John the Baptist learned to walk in Your ways. The road to heaven will always pass through the wilderness.

Drought teaches us to cling to Your word rather than the consolation of Your voice. Drought humbles us. It exposes our weaknesses. Hunger draws forth the darkness that lurks in the recesses of our souls. Silence tests our faith. It requires decision and sacrifice on our part—gifts that we cannot offer in the light of Your presence. When Your consolation floods our souls, our minds are clear. When we hear Your voice, we know there is nothing that compares to Your glory. But when You are silent, we must fight the seduction of the enemy. That fight, I believe, is a worthy sacrifice in Your eyes. Faith exercised in darkness is precious in Your sight.

I have come to believe that drought is a gift from Your holy hand, though it is a risky one indeed. Thirst is not a gift I desire or dare to request. However, I know that it is a good, for You did not withhold the test from Your Only Begotten.

Even for Jesus, drought followed revelation. At His baptism, You parted the sky. Your voice thundered, "This is My beloved Son, in whom I am well pleased" (Matt. 3:17). The Holy Spirit descended on Jesus in the form of a dove. His heart must have burst with joy!

Then the Spirit, which had just descended, drove Jesus into the wilderness. You sent Your Son to suffer hunger and heat and the voice of Satan himself. I believe You kept silent those forty days, like You did at the crucifixion. The test was severe. Yet in His thirst, Jesus clung

fast to Your word. Your word was hidden in
His heart, and it became His food and drink.
It was His armor and His weapon against the
enemy. Your word was Jesus's refuge when
Your voice was silent.

Jesus passed the test that Abraham failed.
The test that the Exodus generation failed.
The test that I too have failed.

Like my father Abraham, I have heard the
Lord's voice. I have been swept off my feet and
intoxicated by His promise. Granted, the word
spoken to me did not carry the cosmic
consequence of the blessing bestowed on
Abraham. Nonetheless, it came from the
mouth of God and, for that reason, I believe it
to be unshakable.

I was lying in bed one night, praying about
a warning I had received from my youth
pastor. He was concerned about my level of
zeal. I had recently had my first encounter with
the Holy Spirit, and for weeks my heart had
been singing with joy. My head was full of
plans for evangelizing my school, organizing
Bible studies, and the like. I wanted nothing
more than to draw others into the giddy
wonder I had found. My pastor worried that
an emotional letdown was imminent and that
my faith would be damaged in the fall. But I
believed that God had deposited a lasting gift
in my soul, so I dared to ask, "Is it true, Lord,

that this feeling will go away? Can't I always be this close to You?"

You heard me, and You answered with a word that shook me to the core. While I was praying with my head toward the exterior wall of my room, I felt a Presence enter through the door. I dared not look, for I knew what I would see. There was a man standing beside my bed. He was tall and mighty, powerful beyond comprehension. My heart beat fast. I could hardly breathe. I blinked my eyes to make sure I was awake and not dreaming, but I had no doubt. I had never felt more alert, or more afraid.

I felt Jesus's hand slide underneath me, lifting me up, though my body remained on the bed. I was suspended in His grasp, and the sensation was both wonderful and terrifying. He released me and spoke words that I can neither forget nor deny— "Nothing will ever take You away from Me."

I told no one about that encounter for years. I felt no need to do so. I did not write the message in a journal lest I forget. The word was etched in my soul. I pondered that encounter daily for months, full of wonder and awe. I could not wrap my head around Your humility. Why would you bother to speak to an unremarkable teenager in Texas? But you did! And I was terrified that You would come again that way. Like the Israelites who heard Your voice in the wilderness, I begged You never to speak so directly again, for I did not know if I could survive another meeting like that one.

Once again, You answered my prayer. I have never seen you like that again.

My drought began just weeks after this encounter. It was not a physical hunger that afflicted me, but a harsh discovery of the lust of my flesh. For the first time in my life, I came face-to-face with the impotence of my will, and my utter dependence on God's grace. For seven years I wandered through a spiritual wilderness, acting in ways inconsistent with my belief. I looked to young men to satisfy the cravings of my soul. My mind was filled with thoughts I hated. My only hope was that You knew how miserable I felt, for I never stopped loving You. I never forgot the thrill of Your voice. I was always drawn to Your holiness, even in the midst of my sin.

In that wilderness, Your word became the anchor of my soul. I pored over Scripture, memorizing Your promises of forgiveness. I clung to the word I heard in my bedroom—that nothing would ever take me from Jesus's hand. I put those words on my lips in prayer. I dared to hope that "nothing" included my own sin. I prayed that Your love for me was stronger than the weakness of my flesh. And like Abraham, I learned that it was.

Six years into my drought, one day I was reading John chapter 10, where I discovered that the word I heard was given to all of Jesus's disciples.

> My sheep hear My voice, and I
> know them, and they follow Me.
> And I give them eternal life, and
> they shall never perish; neither
> shall anyone snatch them out of
> My hand. My Father, who has
> given them to Me, is greater than
> all; and no one is able to snatch
> them out of My Father's hand. I
> and My Father are one.
>
> —John 10:27–30

I knew then that I had heard correctly! The word had substance. It could be received in faith.

Soon after this discovery, Lord, You set me free. The release came as suddenly and unexpectedly as the test had begun. You purified my mind. You enabled me to follow my Good Shepherd once again on paths of righteousness. I came out of the drought a wiser, more humble sheep. You did not abandon me, nor let me starve to death.

During the years of drought, I clung fast to my spiritual fathers. Countless times I read Paul's lament over his own weakness (see Rom. 7:7–25). I remembered Your love for David, even in his sin. I looked to Your mercy toward Abraham and found courage to keep plodding forward. It comforted me to know that the father of many nations stumbled, yet never lost Your promise.

Drought often follows on the heels of revelation. This is Your wisdom, Lord. When we are weak, when we despair because of sin, we must hold fast to Your word. We learn that Your love outweighs our failure—and this truth steadies the heart more than any ecstasy.

# 4

# LOT

*Abram said to Lot, "Please let there be no strife
between you and me, and between my herdsmen and
your herdsmen; for we are brethren. Is not the whole
land before you? Please separate from me. If you take
the left, then I will go to the right; or, if you go to the
right, then I will go to the left."*
*—Genesis 13:8–9*

*And Lot lifted his eyes and saw all the plain of Jordan,
that it was well watered everywhere (before the LORD
destroyed Sodom and Gomorrah) like the garden of
the LORD, like the land of Egypt as you go toward
Zoar. Then Lot chose for himself all the plain of
Jordan, and Lot journeyed east. And they separated
from each other.*
*—Genesis 13:10–11*

WHEN ABRAHAM SET OUT from his father's house, he took Lot with him. I wonder why? Scripture does not indicate that You instructed Abraham to do so, but nor did You object. Did Lot ask to join his uncle, or was it the other way around? Either way, it seems Abraham felt a fatherly duty toward his brother's son.

The writer of Genesis informs us that Abraham had two brothers. One of those brothers, Lot's father, Haran, died an untimely death in Ur of the Chaldeans. The text suggests that Lot may have been young at the time of his father's passing, for when Abraham's father, Terah, moved away from Ur, he took Lot and Abraham with him. The land where they settled next was called Haran. Did Terah name the land in honor of his lost son? The text does not explain. We know only that Lot was invited to join his uncle's pilgrimage to Canaan.

Both Abraham and Lot were wealthy when they departed Haran. They took "all their possessions that they had gathered, and the people whom they had acquired" (Gen. 12:5) to the land of Canaan. The drought that struck soon after their arrival propelled a huge caravan of people and animals to Egypt. Lot witnessed God's judgment on Pharaoh for taking Sarah as a wife. That would be enough to make me fear my uncle, but Lot seemed to miss the point.

When Abraham and Lot came up from Egypt, their combined flocks had grown so numerous that the land could not support them. Abraham's herdsmen began quarreling with Lot's. In order to keep peace in the family, Abraham proposed that the two men part ways.

Abraham offered Lot the pick of the land, which is interesting to me. I think Lot should have deferred to his uncle. Abraham was the prophet. He was the friend of God. He was the one to whom the land was promised. But Lot did not honor his uncle as God did. He did not fear the Lord's hand upon him. Therefore, Lot chose the better land for himself.

Scripture says the plain of Jordan, near Sodom, was well watered and fertile. Life there must have looked enticing to a drought-weary wanderer. It was well known that the men of Sodom were "exceedingly wicked and sinful against the Lord" (Gen. 13:13), but Lot never planned to join in their evil, I assume. He simply saw a great business opportunity—a chance to make a profit and kick up his heels for a bit.

I suspect Abraham was surprised when Lot settled in the city. I imagine he considered his

nephew a fellow pilgrim seeking the promise—
"a city whose architect and builder was God"
(Heb. 11:10). But Lot never showed any zeal
for seeing the promise fulfilled. Maybe he
doubted because he had never heard the voice
of the Almighty. (Even if this were true, the
incident with Pharaoh should have troubled
his sleep.) Perhaps Lot simply resented living
under the shadow of his uncle. Like many
young men, he wanted to stretch forth and
make his own mark in the world.

How tragic! How human! How utterly
relatable is Lot's temptation! Among all the
families on the earth to be blessed in
Abraham's promise, Lot's family would surely
have been first in line. But Lot did not want to
wait for someone else's blessing.

Unwittingly, I think, the Gentile church
has adopted Lot's posture toward the
descendants of Abraham. We have received
the gift of salvation from the Messiah born of
Abraham's line, but we have distanced
ourselves from the biological children of
Abraham. We are eager to call ourselves the
New Jerusalem, but we do not weep for the
land in which Abraham walked.

When we regard our blessing apart from
Israel, we fail to see the magnitude of the story
into which we have been called. We limit our
wonder regarding Your salvation and our

estimation of Your friendship with men.
When we distance ourselves from the full hope
of Abraham—the name, the nation, and all the
families of the earth—we find ourselves in the
same danger as Lot, with pride and seduction
crouching at the door.

Soon after Lot departed, You came to
Abraham again saying,

> Lift your eyes now and look from
> the place where you are—
> northward, southward, eastward,
> and westward; for all the land
> which you see I give to you and
> your descendants forever. And I
> will make your descendants as the
> dust of the earth; so that if a man
> could number the dust of the
> earth, then your descendants also
> could be numbered. Arise, walk in
> the land through its length and its
> width, for I give it to you.
>
> —Gen. 13:14–17

It sounds as if You were happy, Father, to
have Abraham all to Yourself. He was free to
wander through the land You had chosen and
see it through Your eyes. Whereas Lot found
only hardship in the wilderness, Abraham had
eyes of faith. He cherished the ground on
which You spoke. He surveyed the land at

Your direction until he came to the trees of Mamre where he settled and built an altar.

Was it Your will for Abraham and Lot to separate? I tend to think that it was, for important events were precipitated by their parting. However, these stories would not have unfolded as they did had Abraham ceased to care for Lot. Abraham kept a watchful eye upon his nephew, and that pleased You, I believe, for You never cease to love Your wayward children.

Some years after Lot departed, Chedorlaomer, the king of Elam in the east, went to war against the kings of Sodom and Gomorrah. Chedorlaomer marched on the plain of Jordan with four other kings and their armies under his command. Sodom and Gomorrah allied themselves with two smaller cities in the region in an effort to defend themselves. The nine armies met in the Valley of Siddim where Chedorlaomer and his armies defeated the four opposing kings. The victors plundered Sodom, taking Lot, his people, and all his possessions captive.

A citizen of Sodom, probably a servant in Lot's household, managed to escape the battle. Aware that Lot's uncle lived by the oaks of Mamre, he went in search of the prophet to inform him of his master's fate. Upon hearing the news, Abraham immediately mustered 318 trained men born in his household. He called on his friends—Mamre, Eschol, and Aner—to summon their men. Then this band of nomads, led by an elderly prophet, chased Chedorlaomer and his five armies, overtaking them near Dan. Abraham's men fell upon the armies at night. They freed Lot and his people, retook the loot stolen from Sodom, and pursued the kings as far as Damascus. That is a distance approximately 150 miles from their starting point. Not bad for an old man!

Lord, You are a warrior who will one day subdue all the kings of the earth! You clothed Abraham in strength as he went to battle for Lot, causing fear to seize his enemies. This victory near the beginning of salvation history serves as a type for the end of the age when Your Son will wage war on Your enemies, setting all the captives free.

But that day will not come without warning. It has been long foretold. You have invited us to repent. And there will be further signs, I am certain, before that great and terrible day dawns on earth. In the same way, I think, You were calling to Lot. You were commanding Sodom's attention with Chedorlaomer's attack. Sadly, neither Sodom nor Lot repented. Thus, You invited Abraham to intervene once more.

You paid a visit to Your friend as he rested near the oaks of Mamre. Genesis 18 says that You appeared to Abraham as he sat by the door of his tent in the heat of the day. Immediately, he recognized Your presence. He knew Your voice. He easily discerned You in the three visitors who suddenly appeared in his camp. Bowing before You, the One-in-Three, he begged You to tarry as he prepared a meal.

No one else in Scripture ever encountered You in visible, Trinitarian form. No one else has heard with human ears the Persons of the Godhead deliberate among themselves! But You were making Abraham into a great nation, one that would walk in Your ways; thus You allowed him, for a moment, to listen to Your counsel—Father, Son, and Spirit—interacting. Abraham heard You consider the fate of Sodom. He heard you weigh the cries that had ascended to heaven. He heard You execute judgment on behalf of the oppressed. And when You revealed Your intention toward Sodom, Abraham realized that his beloved nephew was in danger.

The prophet dared to challenge You with these questions:

> Would You also destroy the
> righteous with the wicked?
> Suppose there were fifty righteous
> within the city; would You also

destroy the place and not spare it
for the fifty righteous that were in
it? Far be it from You to do such a
thing as this, to slay the righteous
with the wicked, so that the
righteous should be as the wicked;
far be it from You! Shall not the
Judge of all the earth do right?

—Gen. 18:23–25

Abraham understood the audacity of
engaging the Almighty. He posed his questions
in fear and reverence, knowing he was but dust
in Your presence. Once again, he dared to risk
his life for the sake of his nephew Lot.

I believe You delighted in his boldness!
Abraham's challenge proved that he knew
You. He honored You as Judge of the earth,
and he believed You to be righteous. A
righteous judge must differentiate between the
wicked and the just. A nation that would walk
in Your ways must do the same. You allowed
Abraham to keep narrowing the number for
which You would spare the city, exploring
Your thoughts, advocating for life.

Abraham had spoken with You many times
before. He had interceded for Pharaoh at Your
direction. But this type of prayer was new for
him. He was acting like Your Son, pleading
mercy for a soul in danger. In doing so, he

began to walk in his calling as a blessing to the nations. He took on the role of a spiritual father to Lot, a man who would never be counted as a member of the promised nation for he was not a direct descendant. And not only did Abraham intercede for his nephew; he cried out for justice on behalf of any righteous soul that could be found in the city.

In that most holy encounter, Abraham was relating to You as You hoped man would from the beginning. You created man in Your image so that he might know You and be known. Abraham knew You to be just, as You knew Abraham to be merciful. Someday all those saved by Your Son, born of Abraham's line, will stand in the presence of the Godhead. Together we will rule the nations with Jesus. Abraham's children will render just judgments in the light of Your counsel. And You will show mercy to those who have loved Your children.

Though ten righteous people could not be found in Sodom, Your kindness extended beyond what Abraham dared to ask. You made sure that Lot should be spared, sending angels to escort him from the fiery doom.

I sometimes ponder how Lot navigated life in Sodom. He never embraced the sexual depravity of the city. On some level, however, he made peace with the citizens of Sodom. He was known at the city gate, not as a prophet calling the people to repentance, but as a businessman. It was there at the gate of the city that Lot met the angels.

Did Lot recognize the two visitors as angels? He bowed low to the ground in honor. Perhaps he perceived something of their holiness. He knew they were not of Sodom, and because they were human in appearance, he feared for their safety. Lot implored the visitors to stay the night with him rather than sleeping in the square, and this is the one deed recorded in Scripture that demonstrates the righteousness Abraham saw. Lot felt a moral responsibility for the strangers.

Lot's reception of the angels raises another question in my mind. How had he escaped the fate he feared for the visitors when he was a newcomer in town? Did he bribe the men of Sodom with his great wealth? Was Your hand upon him, Lord, protecting in unseen ways? Was he like Abraham in Egypt, unaware of Your favor upon him? Or had morality degenerated so rapidly in Sodom that what had been unthinkable when Lot first arrived was now acceptable? How had choosing to live in that environment warped Lot's thoughts and dulled his faith?

Scripture says that before Lot's household had gone to bed, all the men from every part of Sodom —both young and old—surrounded the house. "They called to Lot, 'Where are the men who came to you tonight? Bring them out to us so that we can have sex with them'" (Gen. 19:5 NIV).

News of two visitors spread through the city, and cries went out for gang rape. It is hard to imagine such evil! It is difficult to fathom how the citizens of Sodom kept from consuming one another! Lot's solution to the threat was horrifying. He offered his two virgin daughters to the mob, to do with as they pleased. (see Gen. 19:8).

Clearly, Lot's fear had taken hold of him. He did not recognize Your presence with Him, Lord. He did not call upon You for help. The possibility of divine intervention never entered his head, though two powerful angels stood at his side.

The repulsive compromise Lot proposed to his fellow citizens was met with contempt. "Get out of our way," they replied. "This fellow came here as a foreigner, and now he wants to play the judge! We'll treat you worse than them" (Gen. 19:9 NIV).

This is a threat that the church must be prepared to hear. When Your judgment comes, we will no longer be able to split our loyalties. Friendship with the world will be impossible. If we wish to be saved, we must cut our ties and flee/run.

I fear that many of Your people relate to You as spiritual nephews rather than as true sons or daughters. Like Lot, they have chosen a life of ease over the rigors of the wilderness. They have traded an eternal, mystical promise for a temporal reward. And in the process, they have grown accustomed to the values of their surrounding culture.

Peace with the world is good for business. And the lies of Satan confuse our thinking. Discernment and righteousness are condemned as judgment. The call to repentance is labeled as hate, when in truth it is a lifesaving mercy. Many well-intentioned people cower in fear, unable to serve as prophets. They are blind to the necessity of the judgment that You must render because You are good and just.

The Lots of this age are dull to this truth, though they have not abandoned faith altogether. They believe in You, Father, and in Your Son, though they do not know You as Abraham did. They do not seek You in the wilderness. They do not shun the ways of the world. They do recognize the honor of being called into Abraham's story. They do not trust in Your jealous protection. They fail to see the angels standing at their sides.

The intercession of prophets buys these believers time. The warfare of the saints rescues them from captivity. They will not be abandoned. However, on the day when Messiah comes to judge the earth, all that they prize will burn. For the sake of Your friends who love them, the Lots of this age will be plucked from the fire. But their loss will be great for their possessions are under the rule of Sodom.

When Jesus was among us, He taught His disciples about the coming judgment by invoking the story of Lot.

> It was the same in the days of Lot. People were eating and drinking, buying and selling, planting and building. But the day Lot left Sodom, fire and sulfur rained down from heaven and destroyed them all.

> It will be just like this on the day the Son of Man is revealed. On that day no one who is on the housetop, with possessions inside, should go down to get them. Likewise, no one in the field should go back for anything. Remember Lot's wife! Whoever tries to keep their life will lose it,

and whoever loses their life will
preserve it.

—Luke 17:28–33 NIV

Father, I am glad You show mercy to men
like Lot! I am thankful, for I have at times
been like him myself. But I would rather be
like Your friend Abraham. I want to be
counted among Your prophets, formed in the
wilderness of Your choosing. I hope to stand
with the company of intercessors, listening to
the counsel of the Trinity, imploring Your
mercy for the world. The favor You grant those
who know You is a grace that covers the Lots
of this world. You love Your wayward children,
even as Abraham loved his nephew, and they
will be saved on the day Your Son wages war.

# 5

# MELCHIZEDEK AND THE KING OF SODOM

*And the king of Sodom went out to meet him at the*
*Valley of Shaveh (that is, the King's Valley), after his*
*return from the [a]defeat of Chedorlaomer and the*
*kings who were with him.*
*Then Melchizedek king of Salem brought out bread*
*and wine; he was the priest of God Most High. And he*
*blessed him and said:*
*"Blessed be Abram of God Most High,*
*Possessor of heaven and earth;*
*And blessed be God Most High,*
*Who has delivered your enemies into your hand."*
*—Genesis 14:17–20*

FATHER, I FIND THIS ENCOUNTER between Abraham, Melchizedek, and the king of Sodom one of the most enigmatic stories in Torah. Scholars have puzzled over it for millennia. The character of Melchizedek is particularly mysterious. The text in Genesis offers no clues about his history, nor do later books of the Tanakh expound upon his blessing. If it were not for David's prophetic psalm, this kingly priest of God Most High would disappear from the annals of Israel's history. But You assured that would not happen. Something close to Your heart transpired that day in the King's Valley, something crucial to salvation history. The full meaning of this story is beyond my depth. Much of its import, I sense, is intentionally shrouded in mystery, still waiting to be revealed. Even so, I hope You will be blessed as I ask Your Spirit to help me contemplate that day and what it meant to You.

The beginning of every great story is determined by its end. Authors decide carefully which characters should open a tale. Symbols introduced in early chapters take on greater, more complex meanings as a tale progresses. Foreshadowing missed on first reading becomes clear in hindsight. This is the writer's craft that the great authors have learned from You, Father, a storyteller like no other! You create a living drama in which all humans participate. Some volunteer willingly to be heroes; others are called and appointed. Still others oppose Your chosen ones, playing their parts as villains. Most of the time we simply serve as witnesses—watching, pondering, lending a hand, or crying out for help—as Your great drama unfolds. Each actor is completely free, so the drama is fluid. But the motion of the story flows steadily toward the end You intend.

You chose Abraham as Your first hero—a pivotal character on which the entire story of salvation turns. Because Abraham opens Your drama, he has no knowledge of Your symbols, no recollection of Your mighty deeds, no stories of prophets or saints to help him interpret his own experience. He cannot see the climax of the story in which he acts, nor does he have a peek at its end, as do we. He is moving by faith alone, and his blindness contributes to the tension of the narrative. Abraham cannot fathom the profound prophetic significance of his actions, and that is a mercy. His limited sight preserves his freedom and authenticity before You. Perhaps that is true for all of us—that our limits set us free.

When Melchizedek makes his entrance onto Your stage, Abraham is attending to the aftermath of war. He has defeated five armies and freed their captives. He has seized the booty pillaged from Sodom. He is the victor in control of the spoils who must decide what to do next. Apparently, the king of Sodom calls for a meeting to discuss the matter, and the priest of God Most High is invited to officiate.

Like other biblical stories, this encounter is both a historical event and a prophetic sign. That is Your way, Father. Attending to the necessities of our physical lives always carries spiritual implications. A cup of cold water offered in Jesus's name is recorded in the court of heaven. Yet this story seems more allegorical than most. It is the prefiguring of a revelation that has, in some sense, already played out. And still, my heart tells me there are facets to this mystery yet to be unveiled in the fullness of time.

The names assigned to Melchizedek leave no doubt concerning his dignity. The titles he bears are names most properly assigned to Your Son. Melchizedek (*Melek-Tsedeq*) is identified as a priest of God Most High. He is also the "king of Salem," presumably Jerusalem, the city where Messiah will reign. *Salem* is Hebrew for "peace." *Melek* means "king." *Tsedeq* is translated as "righteousness." Thus, the King of Peace is also the King of

48

Righteousness. It takes no esoteric learning to decipher these names.

Sodom, on the other hand, means "burning" or "scorched." Sodom's king's proper name is Bera, which scholars interpret as "son of evil." Bera's ally, the king of Gomorrah, is named Birsha, "son of iniquity." Thus, Abraham is placed in-between a priest representing Messiah and a king in the sway of Satan. High drama must surely ensue.

Melchizedek moves first in this scene, which is fitting. He is Your priest, and You are directing this encounter. Melchizedek arrives with a plan and two simple gifts—bread and wine. I do not know what symbolic significance those gifts held for Abraham. Two thousand years later, in the hands of Your Son, bread and wine would become instruments of an unfathomable, living blessing. But Abraham does not know what will be.

Melchizedek offers the bread and wine to Abraham, and then blesses him. "Blessed be Abram of God Most High; Possessor of heaven and earth" In the same breath Melchizedek blesses You, Father, giving You glory for Abram's victory. "Blessed be God Most High who has delivered your enemies into your hand."

I find it beautiful, Lord, that You receive blessing in Abraham's victory. If it were not for Your great humility, such mutual blessing would not be possible. Abraham in his flesh can add nothing to Your glory, but You receive his victory as a gift. You delight in the fierceness of his love for Lot. You fill his frame with supernatural strength to put powerful kings to flight, and in their defeat, You are exalted.

Father, I have often wondered at these words that appear so frequently in the psalms: "Bless the Lord, O my soul!" I have sung those words thousands of times, for it feels right, even necessary, to bless You. But how is it that my soul can bless You? As the writer of Hebrews explains, "And without doubt the lesser is blessed by the greater" (Heb. 7:7 NIV). That makes sense to me. It is Your blessing that bestows life, health, wisdom, hope, and salvation. I have no such gifts to give You. And yet, You receive my blessing.

Melchizedek knew that You would receive his blessing. He blessed You in the same breath that he blessed Abraham. In so doing, he pointed toward Jesus, the Great High Priest, who serves as mediator between God and man. Jesus is the only priest who, in words of Job, "may lay his hand on us both" (Job 9:33).

How did Abraham respond to
Melchizedek's blessing? Presumably he took
the bread and wine. Here, Father, I know that
I am swimming in waters too deep for me, but
please allow me to ponder. In a mystical sense,
I see dimly that Abraham's reception of
Melchizedek's cup was a prophetic
participation in the cup of salvation that Jesus
offered His apostles. Scripture informs us that
the patriarchs, in hidden ways, shared in
Christ's redemption. Paul states confidently
that You preached the good news to Abraham.
Paul writes that all the Israelites who passed
through the sea "were baptized into Moses";
furthermore, he continues, they "all ate the
same spiritual food, and all drank the same
spiritual drink. For they drank of that spiritual
Rock that followed them, and that Rock was
Christ" (1 Cor. 10:2–4). I confess I do not
know what it means to be baptized into Moses.
Nor do I understand fully what "spiritual food
and drink" may be. But Paul's words about
Christ present in the Rock are unambiguous.
He clearly indicates that the spiritual drink
that flowed from the Rock, while not the same
as the blood of Christ offered in His death,
bears some kinship to Christian communion.

If this is true, and if the church is built on
the foundation of apostles and prophets held
together in Jesus, then it seems fitting that

Abraham, the father of all Your people, should be offered a type, or a pre-figure, of the gift that would save him and all his children. I see the symbols and rejoice at Your love for Abraham. You preached the good news to Your friend and sent Your priest to feed him with bread and wine.

When Abraham had taken this gift from Melchizedek, he returned a gift of his own. Scripture says that Abraham gave a tithe of all he owned to Melchizedek (see Gen. 14:10). That gift was an act of thanksgiving to You, God Most High.

I cannot imagine what a spectacle that tithe must have been! There was no cash in those days to make such transactions easy. Abraham's immense wealth consisted of sheep and cattle, servants and warriors, fabrics, perfumes, and spices. In addition to his own wealth, when he arrived at the King's Valley, he carried Sodom's treasures in tow. What a glorious procession that tithe must have been! What a witness to Your favor upon Your friend!

All the while, the king of Sodom looked upon the caravan, stewing in his envy, malice, and pride. Bera came with no gift to offer Abraham, nor one for Melchizedek. He did not bless Your prophet or Your priest. He did not thank Abraham for freeing the citizens of

Sodom taken captive in battle. He did not acknowledge Abraham's military feat in any way. Instead, King Bera spoke to Abraham condescendingly with the intention, it seems, of ensnaring him: "Now the king of Sodom said to Abram, 'Give me the persons, and take the goods for yourself'" (Gen. 14:21).

King Bera was a man deep in Satan's grip. Any man who presided over such depravity had to be. Perhaps Bera's offer was a ploy to appear more magnanimous than Melchizedek, who brought only bread and wine. Satan had used that tact before, when he spoke through the serpent in Eden. He accused You, Father, of withholding a desirable gift from Eve, one that he could show her. Of course, the tree of the knowledge of good and evil was not Satan's to give. He had not created it. But he enticed Adam and Eve to reach out and take that which would kill them.

Satan would use this scheme again in tempting Your Son. He laid before Jesus all the kingdoms of the world and offered them to Him if only Jesus would fall down at his feet. The irony of this story is that You had already promised the kingdoms of this world to Your Son. They were His because Your word is certain. Although Jesus knew He must suffer before taking His throne, His flesh surely found Satan's offer enticing. But such an exchange would have been, in fact, an unthinkable transfer of authority. Jesus chose the cup that You offered, Father. By honoring and worshipping You alone, He was able to offer the cup of salvation to His human brothers and sisters.

The king of Sodom pulled from Satan's playbook by offering Abraham what he already possessed. Abraham arrived at the valley of Shaveh with Sodom's loot in tow. But King Bera would not bow to Abraham. He refused to acknowledge his debt to the prophet. Instead, he posed as a selfless king interested only in the well-being of his citizens. Bera insisted that he cared nothing for treasures stolen from his city; he wanted only to see his people returned. And with those words, Satan, the power behind Sodom's throne, tipped his hand. Satan, in truth, cares nothing about worldly wealth. He uses it only a snare for souls.

Abraham responded as a true prophet, and a guide for the faithful in ages to come. He refused to touch King Bera's filthy treasure. Rather, he accepted Melchizedek's cup and bowed to receive his blessing. Then Abraham paid a tithe to a priest who served as a type of Christ. The writer of Hebrews contends that Abraham carried Levi, and all the tribes of Israel, in his loins when he paid this tithe. I believe he also carried his spiritual children in his heart.

Father, this choice Abraham made is one all Your children must face. We must choose between the cup of Your blessing and the lure of Satan. Jesus has offered us eternal life in union with the Godhead! Every spiritual blessing is already ours! But do we have eyes to see this truth? Can I, like Jesus, take up my cross and endure the wait?

Sometimes, Father, it is hard to anchor our hope in the promise because our days on earth pass quickly. We can grasp only a hint of the pattern that You are weaving in our lifetime. Yet You have sworn to bring this great drama to a glorious end. All loose threads will be tied into the glorious tapestry. The meaning of every symbol will be revealed. Each actor will see how his or her role relates to others, and we will rejoice in Your wisdom!

As the story draws to its end, Your Spirit will call us back to its beginning. The portent of ancient signs will illuminate an impending darkness. The witness of history will root Your people as the world begins to shake. Demonic spirits once again will rouse kings to assemble for war, and they will see a great sign (see Rev. 16:14). "Babylon the Great," a city known as "the mother of harlots and of the abominations of the earth" (Rev. 17:5), will meet a quick and violent end. The hearts of the armies assembled for war will melt, for "the kings of the earth have committed fornication" with "the great harlot" (Rev. 17:1–2). Smoke will rise from her ruins, as it once did from Sodom and Gomorrah. Rulers of the earth will see and lament. But before this judgment is executed, You will send an angel to implore, "Come out of her, My people, lest you share in her sins, and lest you receive her plagues" (Rev. 18:4). You will not forget Abraham's plea on the day of Your wrath. You will not wipe out the righteous with the wicked. You will rescue the Lots at the end of this age from the fall of Babylon the Great.

Then Your Son will ride out on a white horse and defeat the kings of the earth. The armies of heaven will ride with Him, striking down the armies of evil. In that day an angel will call on the birds of the air to eat the carcasses of kings, and Jesus's words will be fulfilled. "Where there is a dead body, there the vultures will gather" (Luke 17:37 NIV). Your Son understood the sign of Sodom. He foresaw the end to which it pointed.

After His victory, Jesus will put on His wedding garments. He will assemble Abraham's children for a feast. He will adorn us with jewels and fine clothing; He will feed us with bread and wine. Your will shall be done both in heaven and on earth, in the spirit and in flesh, and Your promise shall find its end.

.

# 6

# BELIEF AND RIGHTEOUSNESS

*After these things the word of the LORD came to*
*Abram in a vision, saying,*
*"Do not be afraid, Abram. I am your shield, your*
*exceedingly great reward."*
*But Abram said, "Sovereign Lord GOD, what will You*
*give me, seeing I go childless, and the heir of my house*
*is Eliezer of Damascus?" Then Abram said, "Look, You*
*have given me no offspring; indeed one born in my*
*house is my heir!"*
*And behold, the word of the LORD came to him,*
*saying,*
*"This one shall not be your heir, but one who will come*
*from your own body shall be your heir." Then He*
*brought him outside and said, "Look now toward*
*heaven, and count the stars if you are able to number*

59

> *them." And He said to him, "So shall your*
> *descendants be."*
> *And he believed in the LORD, and He accounted it to*
> *him for righteousness.*
> *—Genesis 15:1–6*

THIS WAS IT—THE MOMENT Abraham became my father. Before he was circumcised, before Ishmael or Isaac were born, You, My Lord, showed Your friend the stars and he dared to believe. I was there that night, I think, twinkling in Your eyes, hidden in the darkness of time. My life was certain because You foresaw it, and Abraham grasped this truth. There were countless offspring hidden in Your heart waiting to call him father. Thus, he placed his hope in Your knowing and his body at Your service. This is true faith, and true righteousness.

For most of my life, I struggled to grasp the link between faith and righteousness. The two looked like different animals to me. Faith I imagined as an invisible reality residing in the mind. Faith, I was told, consisted of embracing correct doctrine and rejecting what was false. Faith was the key to pleasing you, I heard. But that presented a problem to my young mind.

How could I possibly believe all the right things about One who is Transcendence? The fullness of Your truth lies beyond my comprehension. What I believe about You is important, to be sure, for it shapes the way I respond to Your word. But my mind is too small to grasp reality as You see it. My body is too frail to enter Your world. You have set limits on human understanding, and in a way, it is precisely those limits that enable faith to operate. As the writer of Hebrews says, "Now faith is the substance of things hoped for, the evidence of things not seen" (Heb. 11:1).

I have met many men and women of faith who differ from me when it comes to doctrine. We cannot all be correct, for some tenets of our faith contradict one another; yet, we sense a kinship in spirit. The faith we share is not an abstract set of intellectual affirmations; rather, it is an anchor of hope in the God of Abraham, Isaac, and Jacob. Hope, in turn, informs the way we live, and in this regard, we hold much in common.

The connection between faith and ethics has always made sense to me. What we believe about You and Your expectations demands a response. Righteousness, therefore, seemed to me a matter of meeting Your moral standards. If faith were seated in the mind, I reasoned, then righteousness must spring from the will. But there were two problems with this paradigm of mine.

To begin with, the human will proves just as weak as the intellect. In the words of Paul, all of us humans, at some point, "do the very things we hate." Even Your closest friends, Father, struggled in this way. Moses offended you in the wilderness. David, the man after Your own heart, committed adultery and murder. Peter denied Jesus. Even Abraham seemed to lose faith. The whole affair with Hagar and Ishmael looked neither faithful nor righteous to me—but I knew from Scripture that You weighed the matter differently.

You counted Abraham's faith as righteousness. This was the second problem with my paradigm. In Your eyes faith and righteousness seem mysteriously intertwined. Moses was prevented from entering the Promised Land because of his sin, but You never ceased to speak with him face-to-face. David, likewise, was punished for his sin, but You never withdrew Your affection nor Your promise to his descendants. Jesus confronted Peter's denial but went on to vest him with His own authority, empowering him to work wonders. There must have been something about the faith of these men that moved You deeply! Their trust in Your word, their pursuit of Your glory, bound them to You, the Faithful and Righteous One.

The more I ponder the link between faith and righteousness, the more I am astounded, Lord, at the way You entrust Yourself to friends on earth—the way You prove Your righteousness through their faith. Or it could be said the opposite way as well. Your faithfulness is proven by their acts of righteousness. I am not sure I could have grasped the connection between Abraham's belief and righteousness if I had not witnessed a similar story of faith in the life of my own friend. For this privilege, Father, I am forever grateful.

I will never forget the day Caroline told me about Your visitation. The two of us were meeting each week to pray in that season. As soon as she walked into church early one morning, I knew something prodigious had transpired. She was glowing, even shaking, under the weight of Your favor. Before I could ask, she informed me that You had spoken to her a few days earlier, telling her that she would bear another son, a child born of her own body, who would preach the gospel among the nations.

I was terrified at this good news, not because I doubted, but because I knew my friend had been changed forever. Her faith had always been more than an abstract set of beliefs. She was a woman who walked in Your counsel. But now she had received a promise. She had heard Your voice. If she did not see the promise fulfilled, I did not know how her faith could survive. She would either question her own sanity or doubt everything she had come to believe about You.

Caroline responded to Your word in the same way that Abraham did. She opened her body to Your will. She and her husband tried to conceive, just as Abraham and Sarah tried. But unlike Sarah, my friend became pregnant quickly. Then a few weeks later, she lost the baby. Again, she conceived and miscarried. Eight times she opened her womb to receive the child of promise, and eight times she was crushed with disappointment.

Lord, You know how I pleaded with You each time my friend became pregnant. And You know how my heart fell with each death. I had not received the promise myself, but I feared for my friend. I did not know how many times her body or her heart could recover from such loss. I did, however, know that You were able to watch over a pregnancy until birth. I knew You could vindicate the trust of a heart that loved You so truly. I believed You were watching, but You did not intervene.

During those years, I never dared to ask Caroline if she still believed in the promise.

The answer was evident in her action. She chose to keep trying, and so I kept praying. She did tell me, at times, that she wondered if she had failed. Had she done something that prevented the promise from coming to fruition? I imagine that Sarah entertained similar thoughts.

I prayed that You would reassure my friend. I begged You to speak clearly once again, to either encourage or redirect her, and put an end to this trial. After a decade of waiting, You did just that.

Caroline was lying on the couch one morning, feeling sick, pregnant for the ninth time since receiving her promise. In the depths of her heart, she was calculating the time until the expected miscarriage, thinking the coming ordeal would at least release her from the fatigue and nausea of early pregnancy. These were the thoughts you interrupted with a gentle rebuke.

"You have not asked me for the life of this child," You reminded her.

I cannot imagine how those words must have hit her heart. Surely, she assumed, You knew her desire. It was not as if she had never asked for such mercy before. Did she recall the many times such prayers had gone unanswered? Or was she simply relieved to hear Your voice? I only know that she heard You and she responded in obedience, asking for the life of her child.

Caroline did not miscarry that week. Nor the week after. A few months later, at the venerable age of forty-two, she delivered a healthy ten-pound baby boy. There was no doubt in that moment that this child was Your idea. You had done what doctors believed would never happen. You proved Yourself faithful to Your word, and You vindicated Your daughter's belief.

Father, I am astounded at the risks You take with Your friends! Not many souls, I think, are able to endure such long-suffering hope. Not many hearts dare to believe that You speak and that Your word is certain. But how You love those who do! Your righteousness and theirs become one single work. Their faith and Your faithfulness move hand in hand. You reveal through Your holy ones Your intention to save and draw near to us mortals. How could I, as a witness to such faith, ever doubt that Your hand is upon this child of promise? How could Abraham and Sarah, holding Isaac in their arms, ever doubt Your favor?

I am coming to believe there is no such thing as abstract faith. Mental assent to theological principles means nothing to You.

Nor does cold ethical excellence, for that matter. What moves You is belief that You will do the impossible if we simply do what You ask, faith that You are drawing a people to Yourself and making us holy. This, I think, is the kind of faith Abraham, Moses, David, Mary, and Peter possessed. It is a belief that cannot be ruined by moments of doubt, indiscretion, or even moral failure. A person of faith will hope in Your mercy and run after the promise again.

By contrast, there are people who see Your wonders and persist in their doubt. This is why Your anger burned against the Israelites who begged to return to Egypt. They had witnessed Your faithfulness time and again. They had been the subject of unprecedented marvels. All the nations around them trembled because Your glory was upon them. Yet they doubted Your affection, and their doubt became their iniquity.

Pondering the faith of Abraham calls me to consider my own faith. Which of Your promises do I hold most dear? Which of Your words rivet my attention and call me to action? Are there promises, perhaps, to which I am blind or ambivalent?

Your promise to Abraham, I have come to understand, is also a word to me. It ranges far beyond my comprehension, but my greatest hopes are tied to it. My desire to know You and to dwell in Your presence are bound to this promise. So how should I respond?

I find myself praying for the joy of Abraham to be made full, for he is my father and Your friend. I pray for the descendants of his flesh with the same wonder I pray for Caroline's son. And in my prayers, I watch for the fullness of Your promise concerning the land. The completion of all You intend, no doubt, will look different from what I can envision. But I know this hope will not disappoint. Your ways are always broader, greater, deeper, and truer than human imagination.

I respond to Your promise by affirming that Your moral instructions are good. I run after Your ways with joy. I am thrilled to believe that You truly want those You love to be holy.

As a Catholic, I respond to the promises of Jesus by participating in communal rituals. The sacraments of baptism, communion, and confession are acts of faith that bind us to the righteousness of our Savior. They bind us to one another as well, forming us into a people of faith.

I find it interesting, Lord, that You responded to Abraham's faith by making covenant with him. You gave him an action by which to lay hold of Your word. You gave him a rope of obedience with which he could tether himself to You, the Faithful One. The covenant You established with Abraham would extend to his sons as well. You gave them a sign by which they as a people could exercise belief and enter into righteousness.

# 7

# COVENANT

*But Abram said, "Sovereign LORD, how can I know that I shall gain possession of it [the land]?"*
*So the LORD said to him, "Bring me a heifer, a goat and a ram, each three years old, along with a dove and a young pigeon."*
*Abram brought all these to him, cut them in two and arranged the halves opposite each other; the birds, however, he did not cut in half. Then birds of prey came down on the carcasses, but Abram drove them away.*
*As the sun was setting, Abram fell into a deep sleep, and a thick and dreadful darkness came over him. . . . On that day the LORD made a covenant with Abram and said, "To your descendants I give this land, from the Wadi of Egypt to the great river, the Euphrates."*
*—Genesis 15:8–12, 18 NIV*

FRIENDSHIP WITH YOU CAN BE TERRIFYING, Lord. You know this, I am sure. It cannot be helped. Our dust trembles in the presence of the One who is a consuming fire.

Has there ever been a prophet unshaken by Your call? Moses hid his face when You spoke from the burning bush. Isaiah cried out in dread as Your presence shook the temple. Job covered his mouth when You came in a whirlwind. Peter begged Jesus to depart when he witnessed the miraculous catch of fish. Paul fell off his horse blinded by an encounter with Your Son.

Fear marks our psyches in ways that consolation cannot. Holy trembling rattles us to the core. You are eternal; our lives are but a breath. You hold galaxies in Your hand; we cannot stand before You. The hearts of all men are open to You; we dare not look You in the face.

Holy fear is an antidote to mortal fear. Those who tremble at the sound of Your voice are less likely to cower before men. Fear is also strong medicine for disbelief. When we are quaking, we do not doubt Your existence. Nor do we question Your word. The rational mind holds no defense to its undoing in Your presence.

It was not doubt, but faith, that led Abraham to ask you for a sign. This question follows directly upon Abraham's trust in Your word, which You "accounted. . . to him as righteousness" (Gen. 15:6). He was looking for a physical sign on which to hang this spiritual revelation. You responded by binding Yourself to the promise with a covenant.

Terror accompanied the covenant You sealed with Your friend. Darkness, dread, and otherworldly fear attended this covenant sealed with blood and smoke. You placed a flaming brand upon Abraham's heart, scoring the seed of faith, preparing it to die and sprout.

> As the sun was setting, Abram fell into a deep sleep, and a thick and dreadful darkness came over him. Then the Lord said to him, "Know for certain that for four hundred years your descendants will be strangers in a country not their own and that they will be enslaved and mistreated there. But I will punish the nation they serve as slaves, and afterward they will come out with great possessions. You, however, will go to your ancestors in peace and be buried at a good old age. In the fourth generation your descendants will

> come back here, for the sin of the
> Amorites has not yet reached its
> full measure."

—Gen. 15:12–16 NIV

A strange assurance, to be sure, this prophecy of slavery spoken in darkness. It was surely not the type of sign Abraham had imagined. However, this experience was more than a word or a vision. Terror drew Abram into the gravity of Your promise. Without fully understanding it, he felt the awful cost of his election. As You spoke, You took him on a mystical journey into Egypt, into servitude, and out again through the Exodus. Abram passed through the story of his descendants, feeling in some measure their distress and the price of their deliverance.

I would have no boldness to make assertions about such mysteries if Paul had not set the precedent. He tells us that the Exodus generation experienced a similar proleptic journey marked by darkness and by fire.

> I do not want you to be ignorant
> of the fact, brothers and sisters,
> that our ancestors were all under
> the cloud and that they all passed
> through the sea. They were all
> baptized into Moses in the cloud
> and in the sea. They all ate the

same spiritual food and drank the
same spiritual drink; for they
drank from the spiritual rock that
accompanied them, and that rock
was Christ.

—1 Cor. 10:1–4 NIV

I find it beautiful, Father, that though
Abram lived before the Exodus, and before the
coming of Messiah, he was bound to Your
deliverance in the covenant You established
that day. Your covenant was an oath to bring
the promise to completion, through all the
sacrifice, blood, and agony it would require.
You saw the end from the beginning, and You
drew Abram into Your eternal truth.

When You roused Abram from his deep
slumber (was it similar to Adam's sleep, I
wonder?), he saw a smoking firepot passing
between the halves of bloody carcasses. The
fire did not consume the sacrifice, as the angel
of death did not touch the bloodied doorposts
of the children of Israel. You spoke to Abram
as the fire moved, much as You spoke to
Moses on the night of the Exodus. The
Israelites stood on the shore of the sea,
trembling in terror as the armies of Pharaoh
closed in on them. A God they hardly knew
beckoned them from a pillar of fire to pass
through deep waters. You were with them in
the cloud, as You were with Abram in the

smoke. "He guided them during the day with a pillar of cloud, and he provided light at night with a pillar of fire" (Exod. 13:21 NLT).

Your heart burned with love as Your people passed under the cloud and through the sea. Your heart burned for Abram the night You sealed Your covenant with him. You carried him mystically into the coming deliverance. And he, like his children, shook with fear.

Another glorious day will come in which all Your children will pass through the darkness of death, leaving behind the shackles of sin forever. We will be caught up in the clouds with the Messiah who will return to the land of promise. We will stand with Abraham on a sea of glass mingled with lightning as we sing the song of Moses and the song of the Lamb that was slain. Your covenant with Abraham points forward still, binding all of His children to You until Your promise reaches its culmination (see Rev. 15:2–3).

This is an astounding truth that I can barely comprehend. You have bound Yourself to a man and to His descendants for eternity. Oh, the unfathomable humility of that act! Oh, the dreadful fierceness of Your love! It runs forward and backward through time, gathering all who love You under the blood of covenant. Even we Gentiles are caught up in this love through the blood of Your Son, the Messiah, who passed through a terror of His own.

All Your children partake in one story, in different roles, at different times. All share in the mystery of the Exodus for it burns eternally in Your heart. On the day You called Israel out of Egypt, You bound Yourself to Israel as a bridegroom. That day was both a wonder in itself and the type of the great and terrible day yet to come, when the sky will roll back as a scroll and the One who sits upon the Throne of heaven will be revealed (see Rev. 6:14-17).

Not many of Your children will see that day in the flesh. However, each person You have called must undergo a spiritual baptism—a personal journey through death to life. Spiritual rebirth will ultimately lead to resurrection. Until that time, You give us mortals physical signs of this promise. Abraham passed a night in mystical darkness before You appeared in fire. Joseph was thrown into a dungeon before You raised him to Pharaoh's court. The Exodus generation passed from slavery into freedom. Jonah spent three days in a fish's belly before being returned to the light. Your own Son underwent the true baptism to which all of these mysteries are tied. His is the baptism that gives all death meaning and hope. His is the baptism that gives our sacrament its power.

Jesus was laid in a tomb, descended into hell, then was raised to Your right hand.

Covenant with the Living God will lead us through terror and darkness into life eternal. The fear cannot be helped. Even Jesus dreaded His passage. But the end of Covenant with the Father of lights is salvation and joy eternal.

# 8

# Circumcision

*Abram fell facedown, and God said to him, "As for
me, this is my covenant with you: You will be the
father of many nations. No longer will you be called
Abram; your name will be Abraham, for I have made
you a father of many nations. . . ."*

*Then God said to Abraham, ". . . This is my covenant
with you and your descendants after you, the
covenant you are to keep: Every male among you shall
be circumcised."*

*—Genesis 17:3–5, 9–10 NIV*

## MYSTERY #1

When I was thirty-four years old, I had a vision. Lying awake in bed one night, pregnant with my fourth child, I saw the infant forming in my womb. My attention was drawn to his tiny hand stretched out in the darkness. He was opening and closing his fist. In a flash I understood what You were showing me. The body of my unborn son was developing in Your image. You designed his hand such that it would communicate something about Your Being. You take hold of people, kingdoms, and times the way we take hold of objects. Whatever You hold cannot not be shaken. Whatever You release will fall.

Humans have eyes because we were made in the image of the God Who Sees. We have ears because You hear the cries of all creatures. Our nose represents Your discernment. Our feet run because You are in motion. We have lungs to breathe because You are Spirit. We have a brain to reason because You are Wisdom.

At the center of our bodies beats a heart, pumping blood to every cell. This blood, You say, is the life of our flesh. It feeds each member of the body and cleanses it of toxins. I confess, Lord, I do not understand the mystery

of blood, but this much I know: the blood of
Your Son gives us life eternal.

A bit of Abraham's blood was shed when
he circumcised his flesh. This blood was an
offering to You—a symbol of his life and a seal
of his trust. Abraham's blood, and the blood
of every circumcision, points toward the new
covenant blood of Your Son. Thus, the blood
of circumcision is held in Your heart as a share
in Your Son's sacrifice. Still, Father, I sense
there are more mysteries at work in this
covenant.

Why did You choose such an intimate sign?
Why so bold, yet hidden? Why not mark
Abraham's arm as a sign of Your strength? Or
his forehead as a warning to his enemies? Why
did You choose his reproductive organ? What
were You saying?

There is a more fundamental question that
I have often pondered. How does our sexuality
reflect Your glory? What have You entrusted to
Your children of dust that angels do not
possess? Jesus says that in the resurrection we
shall be like the angels, neither marrying nor
given in marriage. But in this age You have
decreed that it is not good for man to be
alone. You have made us male and female with
the desire to become one flesh and beget
children.

Satan appears to hate this gift. He works hard to pervert the holy image we bear. Perhaps our sexuality is simply an easy target, a vulnerable point of entry—the place where our physical, emotional, and spiritual natures meet. What havoc we wreak with our bodies when they are consumed by lust! What violence and heartbreak have been caused by unbridled loins! Yet, my Lord, You have not repented of the gift.

I believe you risk the power of sexuality because You are a Father. You have never existed without Your Son. Love for Him beats in the center of Your heart. It was Your fatherly love that stirred You to create men in Your image. It was love for Your Son that drove You to redeem us as a bride. Our life, our hope, and our salvation all spring from Your fatherhood. And in your love for us, You have allowed us to become parents as well. In fact, You designed the story of salvation to depend on the begetting of sons.

This is why, I think, the first sign of Your covenant was placed on the organ of fatherhood. In humility beyond grasping, You united Abraham with Your own fatherhood. You claimed his seed as Your own. You sealed his sons' circumcision, giving them a share in Abraham's fatherhood. Salvation would be stored in the seed of Abraham's sons, waiting for the fullness of time. Eventually, the seed would give flesh to Your Son, and His blood would flow for us.

I feel certain that, in the resurrection, Jewish men will bear the mark of circumcision. You said the sign would be an eternal covenant. It is a mark of glory. It is a sign of faithfulness—Yours and Abraham's and his sons'.

Not all of Your children shall be marked in the flesh, but all shall have circumcised hearts. You promised to remove the foreskin over the center of our beings so that we could love You as Your Son does. The thought is frightening. The knife You wield in the Spirit is no less painful than the knife that cut Abraham's flesh. I feel it at work even now. Circumcision of the heart is a stripping of worldly lusts. It is a dispossession of pride and ambition. This spiritual surgery, like its physical counterpart, is a union with the suffering of the Messiah. I struggle to stay put on Your operating table, Lord. Sometimes I get up and run. But I keep coming back, for when my heart is fully Yours, You will write Your Name on my forehead (see Rev. 22:4).

## MYSTERY #2

Here is another mystery, Father—the day You gave Abram the covenant of circumcision is the day You changed his name to Abraham. You made him the "father of many nations" (Gen. 17:4) precisely when You separated him from all other tribes of the earth. This is a mystery of the individual and the universal, the flesh and the spirit, the temporal and the eternal, the visible and the invisible.

We Gentile Christians have a hard time grasping Your interest in Abraham's foreskin because we know You, God, as Spirit. We enter Your family through a mystical rebirth rather than a physical circumcision. The waters of baptism leave no mark upon our bodies. Our spiritual birth, both real and eternal, is the fruit of faith unseen. But our faith is not entirely blind. It rests squarely upon Your faithfulness. You are the God who keeps covenant, and Your covenants are sealed in blood—physical, earthly blood.

The body matters to You. It is Your design. You hold no interest in abstract moral good. You never have. Truth in the heart is impossible without obedience of the body. Your Son made that clear. "The Word became flesh and dwelt among us" (John 1:14), and He was circumcised on the eighth day, according to the law.

No wonder You threatened to kill Moses as he traveled from Midian to Egypt! His son was uncircumcised. You could not entrust a prophet with a new covenant if he would not keep the first. Your threat against Moses was not capricious. It was a matter of Your truth. You had sworn to Abraham to cut off from his people any man who refused to keep the covenant of circumcision. If You failed to keep Your word to Abraham, the blood of his circumcision would cry out for justice. Isaac's and Jacob's blood would prove meaningless should You exempt the Lawgiver from the requirement placed on his forefathers. That could never be. How could the Exodus generation be certain of Your faithfulness to the covenant established with them if You proved indifferent to Your word to Abraham?

The wonders You worked through Moses were, in fact, the fulfillment of Your word to Abraham. Moses led the Israelites out of slavery, just as You foretold. Then You went beyond the promise. You parted the sea in a spectacle of divine power and love. You taught Moses Your ways. You spoke to him face-to-face, as a man speaks with a friend. You told him Your Name. Abraham could scarcely imagine such glory!

The covenant of the Law was a flowering of the covenant of circumcision, not a replacement. It was a movement from glory to glory. Moral instruction was married to sacrifice; love of neighbor went hand in hand with the blood of animals. Under Moses You drew the Israelites close, making them wise as well as strong. Your fame spread to surrounding nations. Rahab and Ruth came to fear You, and You adopted them as daughters. The promise was expanding as You had foreseen, both in flesh and in spirit.

If the glory of the Mosaic covenant surpassed that of circumcision, what can be said of the new covenant sealed with the blood of Your Son? Oh, the depths of Your love for us! Who could have foreseen the end of Your promises, the fruit of all Your covenants? Who could have imagined the riches of the blessings stored up in Abraham's seed? Jesus, the Son You gave, would finally open the gates of Paradise to every family on earth.

I wonder what Jesus felt that night with the cup resting in His hands. What tension He must have felt being both God and man—anticipating the triumphant climax of salvation while dreading the awful test. Surely He held Moses and Abraham in His heart. Just days before, He had met with Moses and Elijah on Mount Tabor. They spoke together of the exodus He would accomplish, descending into hell and leading forth its captives to freedom. What joy they must have shared in that moment! These friends beyond the veil understood that Jesus had not come to abolish their revelations, but to fulfill them.

When the blood of Your Son was shed on the cross, both heaven and earth were shaken. Graves of stone broke open and dead saints walked the streets of Jerusalem. Christ's triumph in the Spirit was manifest in flesh as a token of what will come.

We live in a mystery like Abraham's—bound in time to an eternal truth. Our father's flesh was marked as a sign of a spiritual blessing. Our souls are marked with the blood of our circumcised Savior as a promise of bodily resurrection. There are aspects of Your covenants, Father, that still await their manifestation. The earth is not yet filled with Your knowledge as the water covers the sea. Our minds are not yet fully transformed. Jesus does not yet reign in the flesh from a throne set in Jerusalem. But these promises are certain for You have spoken. In the words of the apostle John, "now we are children of God; and it has not yet been revealed what we shall be, but we know that when He is revealed, we shall be like Him, for we shall see Him as He is" (1 John 3:2).

When we see You, Father, we shall also see Abraham in his glory. Our minds will finally comprehend the wonders of Your ways. The eyes of our new flesh will rest upon the Savior of our souls. And all Your children, from every nation of the earth, will bow low to worship the God who keeps covenant with man.

# 9

# THE NARROW GATE

*Sarai said to Abram, "The Lord has prevented me from having children."*
*—Genesis 16:2 NLT*

WHEN SARAH TOLD ABRAHAM that You, Lord, had prevented her from having children, I believe she was right. You had closed her womb. You closed Rebekah's as well, until the perfect time. I believe You were emphasizing the narrowness of Your plan. Your salvation has always traced its path through a single son. Isaac—not Ishmael. Jacob—not Esau. Judah—not Reuben or Levi or Joseph. David—not Eliab or Abinadab. In every generation there was only one son of promise.

This plan of Yours offends our hearts. It troubles our minds as well. Should there not be a hundred billion paths to You? Why do You favor so few and call others into their blessing? Our reaction to Your wisdom betrays our pride. We lash out against the ones You have chosen, like Cain against Abel. We hate the favored brother, as Jacob's sons hated Joseph. We recoil from bowing before one who shares our flesh and blood. Simple jealousy, I think, lies at the root of historic anti-Semitism. We Gentile Christians have trouble accepting the words of our Savior, "salvation is of the Jews" (John 4:22).

Of course, Father, You do love the whole world! Each child holds a unique place in Your heart. You told Abraham that You intended to bless every family of the earth through him. And Your blessing extends beyond all that we could hope or imagine. The end of salvation is eternal life in Your presence—joy forevermore. But what a long and constricted road You have chosen to bring us home!

Jesus said that those who enter the kingdom of God must be born again. If human birth serves as an image for our passage into the kingdom of God, then we should tremble indeed. There is no tighter journey a person must make in the flesh. A bony head, fourteen inches in circumference, moves through a soft-tissue passage that, under normal circumstances, measures just one inch in diameter. The cervix, which seals the womb, is a mere slit of an opening. The contractions of labor open this slit to a staggering ten centimeters, and still the baby's head is too wide. The required stretch is agonizing for the mother. The journey is perilous for the baby. Countless mothers and children have died in labor.

Even before birth, the way of life is narrow. The genetic codes of both father and mother are split in half and distilled into packages too small to see. Two hundred million sperm vie for entrance into a single egg. Two hundred million! Only one sperm will be chosen. And once the union occurs, only two out of three embryos survive until birth. There is a very real sense in which every person born has won a great lottery. Each life is a marvel. Each genetic union that lives to see the light of day has beat out millions of potential competitors. Yet none of us chooses to be born.

In the same way, those born of the Spirit do not choose You, Father. Rather, Your Spirit calls us and quickens our souls. Your love draws Gentiles into salvation, just as You promised Abraham. However, in order for us to enter, we must pass through a very narrow gate. We come into salvation through the door of Your Son, who serves as both our guide and our path.

Jesus Himself walked the narrowest of roads. He was born to a virgin daughter of Abraham—a way closed to all but You. He was hounded by Herod. Threatened by the Pharisees. Condemned by the Sanhedrin. Abandoned by His friends. Crucified by the Romans and laid to rest in a tomb. Then He rose again and ascended to Your right hand.

This is the way You have set before us. Following Jesus sets us on a path of discipleship, obedience, suffering, and death. It is a journey of faith in You and in Your Chosen One. This way requires us Gentiles to bow down before a Jewish man. It calls us to believe in Your word and trust in Your mercy.

Because entry into Your kingdom is a spiritual birth, the passageway must be tight. This is why, I think, rich men find it difficult to enter. We cannot bring our camels into Your presence. We cannot even arrive respectably clothed. We come naked and exposed, like Jesus on the cross. We come as beggars, like Joseph's brothers, or we will not come at all.

In physical birth, the same hormones that trigger labor in the mother cause a transformation in the child. As the baby is pressed and squeezed, her lungs are emptied of amniotic fluid. She is made ready to breathe the air of her parents' world for the first time. And this, I think, is why You have made the way of salvation so narrow. We must be emptied of our old ways to live in the atmosphere of Your presence. Pride must be squeezed out of our hearts, for You, my Lord, are humble. Suffering must be embraced, for You, my Lord, are long-suffering. We must become merciful for You are merciful, and how can we show mercy unless we bear insult and injury? The way of salvation is death to our selfishness—and ultimately, death to our flesh. In our dying, our true natures will be revealed. We will either lash out against You; or like Jesus, we will commend our spirits into Your hands.

93

I cannot imagine what joy we shall know when this passage is complete! Those who have walked the narrow way will see the light of Your face. The breath of Your holiness will rush into our resurrected lungs. Each child born of the Spirit will, at last, rest in the arms of the Father. The wisdom of Your narrow way will be justified in Your children.

# 10

# HAGAR AND ISHMAEL

*God heard the voice of the lad. Then the angel of God called to Hagar out of heaven, and said to her, "What ails you, Hagar? Fear not, for God has heard the voice of the lad where he is. Arise, lift up the lad and hold him with your hand, for I will make him a great nation."*
*—Genesis 21:17–18*

THE STORY OF HAGAR AND ISHMAEL disturbed me as a child. I did not know how to receive it. In Sunday school, Bible stories were presented as morality tales. The patriarchs and prophets were heroes of the faith—models to be emulated. That made sense to me. However, in this story, neither Abraham nor Sarah acted like heroes. Why was this story even in the Bible? I wondered. It would have made more sense to me to skip over this unfortunate episode and focus on Isaac.

What I failed to understand as a child, my Lord, is that You never intended Your word to be a morality tale. Scripture is given to reveal truth—both about You and concerning the human heart. You are not afraid of truth, for You are truth. You feel no temptation to embellish the stories of Your friends, no need to make them look good for the annals of history. Their faults may grieve You, but they do not threaten You. On the contrary, their weakness shows us that even the prophets need a Redeemer.

The story of Sarah, Abraham, Hagar, and Ishmael is painful, messy, and sadly familiar. Everything about the drama is complex. Each actor plays both oppressor and victim, motivated by temptations common to man—doubt, despair, jealousy, pride, denial, passivity, and contempt. I must admit that I am intimately acquainted with all these motives, though as a child they scandalized me. I thought that surely You could have found a more upstanding couple than Abraham and Sarah to build our faith upon. But my understanding was immature.

When I was young, I assumed that You valued good behavior above all else. I was wrong. You know that true righteousness rests upon faith. Without faith, there can be no great deeds of faith. Thus, You are willing to test our faith, stretching it and repairing its flaws, until it can bear the weight of Your work.

Well before this debacle with Hagar, You found Abraham righteous. You knew his heart. You knew Your friend believed the promise and was doing everything he could to make it come to pass. Sarah, likewise, remained faithful to her husband – setting off across the wilderness by his side, submitting to his crazy schemes to pass her off as his sister, trying year after year to conceive. Sarah's faithful submission to Abraham, I believe, was the essence of her righteousness.

Lord, I must say, I have great sympathy for Sarah. It is hard to imagine how she processed her husband's dialogues with You. We know that she followed him when he heard Your call to leave Haran. Such a move, I would imagine, was harder for her as a woman. It is difficult to find stability when one is a nomad. It is a challenge to believe in a divine calling when one has not heard Your voice directly. Yet Sarah followed Abraham in faith. She walked through the wilderness, through drought, through hope and disappointment with no complaint recorded in Scripture. She submitted to her husband's misguided schemes to deceive Pharaoh and Abimelech. It appears that Sarah loved Abraham, as well as wives are able, and her devotion contributed to her distress.

Sarah wanted Your word to come true for her husband's sake. She longed for Abraham to have an heir. And, I think, she feared his disappointment. In her place, I can imagine worrying that my husband's affection would turn into resentment. Perhaps she worried that she truly was the obstacle—that You had found fault with her. Maybe she was not chosen as he was. If she could think of a way to give him a child, she imagined, then the tension in which they lived would be resolved. The thought was appealing, but false. And You, my Lord, will not abide falsehood.

I can relate to Sarah's fear and doubt. My own fears have, in various ways, led to the same sin that Sarah committed—manipulation conceived in unbelief. Unbelief cannot wait.

Unbelief does not trust. Unbelief relies on itself.

Once disbelief took hold of Eve, she turned rash. Eve could have consulted with You about the serpent's words. You came to walk with her every evening. But she no longer trusted You, nor did she fear You as she should have. In the debacle with Hagar, Sarah and Abraham acted much like our first parents. Abraham should have consulted You about Sarah's plan, but there is no indication that he did. He should have carefully weighed the consequences of taking a concubine, a custom he had shunned all the years of his marriage. He should have called his bride to faith; instead, Sarah's doubt clouded his mind.

In the bitterness of her soul, Sarah blamed You, much like Adam did in the garden. "So Sarai said to Abram, 'See now, the Lord has restrained me from bearing children. Please, go in to my maid; perhaps I shall obtain children by her.' And Abram heeded the voice of Sarai." (Gen. 16:2).

It is a terrifying and beautiful truth, Lord, that You require us humans to make choices in darkness. Part of the darkness is Your design, imposed by limits You set on our understanding. Part of the darkness is the work of the enemy, who whispers words of fear to our souls. Choices made to trust You in this

darkness bear a weight we can scarce imagine.
Faith must, of necessity, operate without sight.
In our blindness, we humans are able to offer
You a kind of honor that angels cannot. This
gift of faith moves You deeply. In fact, it unites
us with You. It allows Your power to flow
through us. And when we choose to trust in
the midst of darkness, we vindicate the risk
you take with humans.

The contrary is also true. When we choose
self-reliance, stemming from doubt or fear, the
consequences are bitter and far-reaching, as
Adam and Eve discovered. By taking the
fulfilling of Your promise into their own
hands, Abraham and Sarah unleashed a
torrent of sorrow. They began by violating the
gift of free will You entrusted to Hagar.
Abraham used Hagar as a means to gratify
Sarah. Hagar was not asked for her consent.
Nor did Sarah plan to honor Hagar's
motherhood. In her heart, Sarah imagined
that the son born of Hagar would belong to
her.

Hagar had her own ideas. Bearing
Abraham's child could raise her status in the
household. She might enjoy more of her
master's wealth and favor. Being young and
desirable, she might begin to receive the
recognition she craved. She might even rival
Sarah in her master's eyes. But such thinking

was folly. Using people for one's own ends, whether master or servant, is a sin; and sin always bears bitter fruit.

Lord, I find it interesting that You did not prevent Hagar from conceiving. You intervened to stop Pharaoh from lying with Sarah. You threatened Abimelech with death for taking Sarah as a bride. In both cases You served Sarah as a shield. You preserved her purity. (Would that she had held fast to the memory of Your protective hand! In that sign she could have seen her importance to You.) But You responded differently when Abraham went in to Hagar. You allowed nature to take its course. You honored his will. You allowed him to make a choice in the darkness of doubt, and his choice would have consequence.

Hagar grew proud in pregnancy. She flaunted her youth and her fertility. She shot looks and breathed words that stung Sarah to the quick. Sarah's handmaid became her rival. The plan failed. Sarah found no place in her heart for Hagar's child; and Hagar held no affection for her mistress. Sin had birthed contempt.

Sarah then accused Abraham of bringing this misery upon her. In fact, she called on You, Lord, to judge between her and her husband. Was Abraham perplexed by her anger, I wonder? Did he resent her bitterness? It was, after all, her plan. But he was the prophet who had chosen passivity. He would not confront Hagar. He did not attempt to make peace. Rather, he washed his hands of the mess and told Sarah to deal with Hagar as she saw fit.

Sarah's hatred took the form of abuse. Scripture says Sarah treated her servant harshly—so harshly that Hagar ran away. She fled pregnant into the wilderness. And there, Lord, You spoke to her. You saw her in her distress. You felt for her. You comforted her with Your promise of blessing. You named her child Yourself. You named him for Yourself: Ishmael, which means "the God who hears." And You sent her home.

Hagar was stunned. And humbled. She could not believe that she had seen an angel of the Lord and lived! She heard You speak, just as her master Abraham had. You took notice of her. You knew her, and You knew her son. You spoke to her about her descendants, not Sarah's. I wonder how she pondered that encounter in her heart. Did she understand her master better afterward? She must have told him and Sarah about the matter, for it is recorded in Scripture.

Hagar obeyed and returned as You instructed. Abraham gave her child the name

You had spoken. And the well where she met
You bore the name she gave You, Beer-lahai-
roi, "well of the Living One who sees me"
(Gen. 16:14 NLT).

Lord, I am deeply moved when I consider
how You cared for Hagar. You were moved by
the distress of a slave girl. You hurt for the one
injured by Your friend. You sought her and
spoke to her directly. Hagar heard Your voice
before Sarah did. You gave her Your blessing,
Your comfort, and Your correction. In the
desert, she encountered the God of
compassion.

You chose not to interfere with Abraham's
choice, but neither were You disengaged from
the test of darkness. Under the stress of
waiting, Abraham chose wrongly. He brought
pain and disorder into his family, but You did
not abandon Your friend. You promised to
leave a blessing where there was pain. This
wound is still not fully healed, though it shall
be in the fullness of time. You will make all
things right, for You love Your friends. You do
not control them, but You walk with them.
You cover them. And those who trust You find
that Your mercy runs deeper and wider than
they can imagine.

You, Father, are the One who takes
responsibility. You carry the weight of the gift
You gave humans, the gift of our free will. You

foresaw the joy this gift would bring You and Your Son, and the whole world, when we freely returned Your love. You also foreknew the devastation our free wills would wreak. You had a rescue plan in place from before the foundation of the world—an answer to all the hurt we would cause. Your Son would bear the weight of our sin, and His victory would make all things new.

You are the One who takes responsibility. I cannot tell You, Father, what consolation this truth brings to my soul! I have come to trust the depth of Your mercy, both toward me and toward the ones I have hurt. In my own darkness, I have tried to manipulate circumstances, just as Sarah did with Hagar. At other times, I have withdrawn in fear or despair, like Abraham, leaving loved ones unaided in their times of need. I cannot undo the choices I've made, nor lessen the pain they have caused. But I am coming to hope, Father, that in the fullness of time, You will compensate generously for the harm I have done because I am Your daughter. You pay for damage inflicted by Your children as they are growing into maturity.

And as we grow, You meet us in our darkness. You call us to faith. You went looking not only for Hagar, but also for Sarah. You saw the pain of her heart as well. You changed her name along with Abraham's and You promised explicitly that she would bear the promised son. Sarah would be the mother of the chosen nation, as surely as Abraham would be its father. You made sure that Sarah could hear the word herself, with her own ears, from Your own mouth. You let her know that You heard her laugh. You assured her that her doubt would not hinder the promise.

Isaac was born one year after Your visit to Sarah. Both mother and father rejoiced, and their doubt was healed. Yet, not all was well, for there was a son conceived in the darkness of unbelief. Ishmael, Hagar's son, grew up in Abraham's household, where he enjoyed his father's affection. Before Isaac was born, Abraham pleaded with You, Lord, that Ishmael would carry the promise. You refused that request, though You promised to bless the boy. Ishmael grew strong and confident, honored within the tents of Abraham.

When Isaac was born, Ishmael felt threatened. He resented his father's affection for Sarah's son. The truth of his illegitimate birth began to sting. He would receive no inheritance from Abraham, through no fault of his own. He began to understand that his mother had been used. He grew angry, and his bitterness bred contempt.

Sarah understood that the situation would never improve. There would always be strife in the house so long as Ishmael viewed Isaac as a rival. Sarah implored Abraham to send Hagar and Ishmael away. This time Abraham was distressed, for he loved Ishmael, and he felt the weight of responsibility toward Hagar and her child. A more mature Abraham did consult with You, Lord. He sought Your word regarding his wife's counsel. You assured him that Sarah was right: he must release Hagar and Ishmael into Your hands; You would provide for them. This was a situation that he could not reconcile. It was beyond his ability to right the wrong he had done. But You promised to take responsibility.

In obedience and sorrow, Abraham sent Hagar with her son into the wilderness, where she had fled thirteen years before. And being a faithful Father, You spoke to her once again. You assured her that You had heard her son's cry. You would bless him as You promised. You would not let them die.

When Your word came to Hagar, she was resting near a well, as she had been the first time; however, she could not see the well. You opened her eyes and she was assured that "God was with the lad" (Gen. 21:20).

Ishmael found You in the desert as well. You were his inheritance, as You were to his father. It seems that Ishmael was reconciled to Abraham as an adult, for when Abraham died many years later, Ishmael and Isaac buried their father together.

I am confident, Father, that Sarah and Hagar are now reconciled. I am certain that Ishmael and Isaac are friends in eternity. And I even believe that despite the pain they endured for a moment, Hagar and Ishmael are both grateful for the roles they played in Your story. They bear witness to a truth greater than any Sunday school lesson. They are recipients of Your compassion. Their stories tell the wonder of Your faithfulness to the victim, the outsider, those outside the promised line. They reveal the depths of Your goodness in ways simple moral models cannot.

I am thankful for Hagar and Ishmael because they instruct me in my own story. You have found me hiding in the wilderness angry, ashamed, afraid—both a sinner and a victim. You have seen us all, and You have sent Your Son to save us, for You are the God of compassion.

I am thankful for the raw, unadorned truth of Your story. I am glad You are not ashamed of the failings of Your friends. You are not ashamed of them, for You carry the glory of their faith in Your heart. You alone know

faith's true value, its weight, its explosive
power in history.

You are not hesitant to display the flaws of
Your prophets, for You know that we need
truth more than good examples. We need to
know You, for You are truth, and Your truth is
revealed in Your story. You are the God Who
Sees. And You are the God who hears. Blessed
be Your Name!

# 11

# SARAH

*Abraham said to God, "Oh, that Ishmael might live before You!"*
*Then God said: "No, Sarah your wife shall bear you a son, and you shall call his name Isaac; I will establish My covenant with him for an everlasting covenant, and with his descendants after him."*
*—Genesis 17:18–19*

*Therefore Sarah laughed within herself, saying, "After I have grown old, shall I have pleasure, my lord being old also?"*
*—Genesis 18:12*

*You have stolen my heart, my sister, my bride.*
*—Song of Solomon 4:9 NIV*

IN ITS FULL REALIZATION, the covenant You established with Abraham will reverse the curse of the garden. Its blessing will heal the rift between man and woman. It will free people from sin, ending slavery in all its forms. Such a glorious gift You would not permit to unfold from an act of sexual coercion.

The covenant was a gift of Your free will. Its reception needed to be free as well. Abraham accepted Your call willingly, as did Mary. Sarah also heard Your promise and presented her body in hope.

The covenant You made with Abraham was a gift of love, conceived in the counsel of the Godhead. You insisted that the promised child be conceived in the union of marital love.

The covenant was a gift of joy—the joy of Your fatherhood. It was fitting that Sarah should feel pleasure in her part of Your plan.

The covenant was the promise of a family vast enough to fill Your Father's heart. You insisted that the family's first son be raised in the fidelity of marriage.

The covenant was a divine intervention in the affairs of men. Your word came unsought, unexpected. Its fulfillment would also be miraculous. You wanted no help from scheming mortals.

It was imperative that Abraham's promised son be born of Sarah, not Hagar, because Sarah was a wife, and Hagar a slave. This, I think, is the most astounding mystery of all. Through the covenant You established with Abraham, You set into motion a plan to form a Bride for Your Son. A Bride who would have authority and honor. A helpmate who would partner with Jesus in His ministry. A Beloved Wife cleansed by His blood. A Bride who would respond to her Bridegroom with desire, not slavish fear. Sarah, not Hagar, is the type of this Bride.

Father, I believe we fail to understand the importance of Sarah in Your plan when we make the mistake of thinking it is all about us humans and our salvation. The covenant was conceived for the joy of Your Son before the foundation of the earth. And this promise that will find its fullness in a Holy Wedding Feast could not rest on an act of sexual exploitation. It had to be born of love.

# 12

# HE LAUGHS

*Then Abraham fell on his face and laughed, and said
in his heart, "Shall a child be born to a man who is one
hundred years old? And shall Sarah, who is ninety
years old, bear a child?"*
—*Genesis 17:17*

*And the LORD said to Abraham, "Why did Sarah
laugh, saying, 'Shall I surely bear a child, since I am
old?' Is anything too hard for the LORD? At the
appointed time I will return to you, according to the
time of life, and Sarah shall have a son."
But Sarah denied it, saying, "I did not laugh," for she
was afraid. And He said, "No, but you did laugh!"*
—*Genesis 18:13–15*
*Then God said: "No, Sarah your wife shall bear you a
son, and you shall call his name Isaac."*
—*Genesis 17:19*

LORD, I HOPE IT DOES NOT SOUND condescending for me to say that I find Your interest in names charming. The sentiment, I realize, reveals my own dullness. We mortals assume that "a rose by any other name would smell as sweet." But that is not true for You. When You speak a word, it comes to life. When You name a man, he is marked with Your calling. Your words carry a power that ours do not.

Naming gives You joy. You could hardly wait, it seems, to show each of Your animals to Adam and ask what he would call them. You delighted in his answers as a father delights in a child's first words.

Naturally, we humans carry some of our Maker's enthusiasm for naming. Important places bear the names of our heroes. Scientific theories carry the names of those who proposed them. Parents deliberate carefully when choosing the name of a child. And the church asks as its first question for every infant presented for baptism, "What name do you give this child?"

Father, I believe You listen more eagerly than any priest for the answer on our lips. You rejoice when we christen our babies with beautiful, affectionate names, for in so doing, we express Your own nature at work in us. The authority to name is a gift You bestowed upon man.

Even so, there have been rare instances when You have claimed for Yourself the right to name a child. In those cases, I think, the name was too important for us to miss. The course of history would turn on the arrival of those babes. You were intervening in human affairs. You had something to say.

"He laughs" is the name You picked for Abraham's son of promise. What a curious choice for the boy who would carry a great nation in his loins! Once again, I must say, Lord, I find it charming, and wonderful, that You would be so lighthearted at such a moment. Who would imagine that the Almighty would enjoy ribbing His friends? Humor is a sure sign of intimacy, and jokes born from a shared history are especially sweet. But I believe there is more to this name. I believe You were looking forward as well as backward.

Every time Sarah called Isaac's name, she remembered her incredulous laughter behind the flaps of her tent. Abraham recalled laughing prostrate in Your presence as You assured him he would have an heir born of his seed. Both parents remembered laughing with joy when Isaac was born, and when he took his first steps, and when he spoke his first words.

All the while, Lord, You were laughing with a joy greater than theirs, because You still had secrets up Your sleeve.

When You speak a word, it is living and active, continually expanding in new angles and depths. You changed Abram's name to Abraham, and the truth of that new name becomes richer, more fully manifest, as time passes. Abram already meant "exalted father." His given name was a prophetic sign of his calling even before he heard Your voice. However, that name must have felt like a cruel mockery for most of his life. I wonder what he thought when You upped the ante, calling him "Abraham," meaning "father of many nations"? I imagine You were laughing, for You knew what You held in store.

Abraham lived to see the first fruits of his new name. Isaac married. Ishmael began to grow into a mighty clan. Abraham married Keturah after Sarah died, and he had more sons. He could see his lineage expanding. However, he never imagined the multitude and diversity of nations that would claim him as their father! Abraham now stands at Your throne, astounded, undone, ecstatic, humbled at the sound "like the roar of many waters" — his children singing Your praise. And Balaam's prophecy concerning the nation that sprang from his loins is fulfilled—"his seed shall be in many waters; his king shall be higher than Agag, and his kingdom shall be exalted" (Num. 24:7 ESV).

When You speak a word, Lord, it is living and active. It becomes deeper, more beautiful, more fruitful over time, like the water flowing from the temple in Ezekiel's vision.

Israel's third patriarch, Abraham's grandson, was called Jacob by his parents. The name means "supplanter"—a fitting moniker for the child who sprang from the womb grasping his older twin's heel. Even before birth, Jacob and Esau wrestled with one another. Esau, the firstborn, was his father's favorite, but You loved Jacob because his heart was set on the promise. Jacob coveted the birthright, whereas Esau despised it, selling it for a pot of stew. Desire is evidence of faith, or at least one's capacity for faith. And desire moves Your heart even in the face of moral failings.

Jacob deceived Isaac to receive his father's blessing, once again acting as a supplanter. His trickery provoked Esau's hatred. Esau planned to kill his brother, so Rebekah warned Jacob to flee. Jacob returned to Haran, the land of Abraham's family, and spent twenty years as a sojourner, building a family and flocks. Then You called him back to the land of promise, the land where his brother dwelled.

Jacob obeyed, though he feared the wrath of Esau. In an attempt to appease his brother, Jacob sent trains of camels and goats ahead of his family, but dread filled his soul. The evening before their meeting, You came to Jacob. You wrestled with him through the night. Once again Jacob proved how he longed for Your blessing, refusing to let go until You blessed him personally. In response, You changed his name. You called him Israel—one who contends with God and with men. How true that name has been! And how difficult to bear. But neither You nor Israel has let go in the struggle, and there is a blessing yet to come.

After Israel wrestled with You through the night, You humbled him by touching his hip. Israel's limp reminded Him of Your blessing, and Your faithfulness. When the night was over, Israel met his brother. The two embraced and wept. They were reconciled.

I believe You have a blessing yet to give Israel, one that will require further wrestling. Someday the children of Israel will recognize their Messiah. On that day, the promise will find its end. We Gentiles will embrace the chosen son, as Esau embraced Jacob, and together we will enter into our Father's house. Perhaps You will change Israel's name again when the years of wrestling are complete. This seems to be Your way, for Your calling is ever expanding, and naming gives You joy.

Jesus changed Simon's name to Peter, sharing with Him His own identity—the Rock of Israel. And once again we marvel at the truth of this name. Two thousand years later, despite attacks from without and failures within, the church founded upon the Rock still stands. She now covers the globe, refreshing the peoples of the earth with living water that continues to flow forth from her inmost being.

Jesus did not change Saul's name when He spoke to him on the road to Damascus. Nevertheless, the great apostle to the Gentiles experienced a shift in the name by which he was commonly known. Like the king who persecuted David, Saul of Tarsus persecuted the Son of David. Yet the Saul of the New Testament was different. You saw something in his heart unlike King Saul's. You recognized the seed of faith that moves You so deeply; so You blessed him by blinding him, by humbling him, that the seed of faith might take root. In the later years of his ministry, Saul became better known by his Latin name, Paul, meaning "humble" or "small." The Latin name was fitting for one working among the Gentiles, a calling he would have despised in his youth. The name was proven by the sufferings he endured—beatings and hunger, rejection and a "thorn in his flesh." The name reflected the truth Paul embodied—that when he was weak, Christ in him was strong. Paul is now humbler than ever as He beholds You, Father, seated in glory with Your Son at Your right hand. Paul is smaller in his own eyes in heaven than he was on earth, but more influential in the annals of eternity than King Saul.

Someday soon You will change my name. A white stone inscribed with a new name known only to the individual is promised to each child of God who overcomes. It will be a living name from Your own heart; a secret name revealing our identity in Your eyes. That name shall become increasingly true throughout eternity, like Abraham's name.

May I tell you, Father, that I find this promise wildly romantic? I am moved to the core to hear that You know me, like You know Abraham, Isaac, and Jacob. I am in awe that You care about the names of Your children, and that You will have the last say on the matter. I quiver at the thought of hearing that secret name on my Savior's lips. I know the name will be spoken in love, and I know it will be true. I will see myself through Your eyes, Lord, and thus I will come to know myself. But what is far, far better and more wondrous yet—

soon I will hear You speak Your Own Name! I will be immersed in Your Name. I will know the glory that Moses longed to see.

That day feels like a fantasy to me, though I know it is present to You. In the same way, Isaac's life was real to You when the hope of his birth felt like a dream to Abraham. You held Isaac's arrival firmly in Your hands because his birth would herald a new day on earth, the first fulfillment in Your plan of salvation. Isaac's birth was proof of Your faithfulness to Abraham, but it was more than that. Isaac was a sign of a secret shared in the counsel of the Godhead. Isaac was the first fruit, a foreshadowing of glorious drama to unfold when a virgin would conceive and bear Your Son, Your Only Begotten. The One You loved would serve as an atoning sacrifice for the whole world. Isaac would participate in the mystery of the Incarnation as both progenitor and prophetic actor. For this reason, Father, I believe You Yourself laughed with joy the day Isaac was born, and You gave him a name that looked to the future as well as the past.

When Gabriel was sent to Mary, he instructed her to name her child Yeshua (Jesus), meaning "YHWH saves." Yeshua came, One in Being with You, to save all who believe. That work is complete. But soon He will return to earth again with a different mission. He will come as Judge, and on that day He will bear a new name known only to Himself.

> I saw heaven standing open and there before me was a white horse, whose rider is called Faithful and True. With justice he judges and wages war. His eyes are like blazing fire, and on his head are many crowns. He has a name written on him that no one knows but he himself.
>
> —Rev. 19:11–12 NIV

Even Jesus will have a new name! And in the day of His wrath, David's prophecy will be fulfilled.

> The One enthroned in heaven laughs;
>    the Lord scoffs at them.
> He rebukes them in his anger
>    and terrifies them in his wrath, saying,
> "I have installed my king
>    on Zion, my holy mountain."
>
> —Ps. 2:4–6 NIV

When Your Son comes in glory, Father, You will laugh in vindication, mocking the arrogant, rebellious rulers of the earth.

Sarah will laugh in wonder to see her Lord and Offspring robed in power. Her ancient prophecy will find its fullness—"all who hear will laugh with me" (Gen. 21:6).

Israel will laugh in awe to see every promise made to the nation realized. They will echo the psalmist: "our mouths will be filled with laughter and our tongues with joyful shouting; as we say among the nations, 'the Lord has done great things for us!'" (see Ps. 126:2–3).

All who mourned on this earth will laugh, just as Jesus promised. You will wipe away the tears of Your children and it will be "as a dream when one awakes" (Ps. 73:20).

Best of all, Your own Son, Your Only Begotten, Your Isaac, the Sower who planted His life as a seed in the ground, "shall doubtless come again with rejoicing, bringing his sheaves with him" (Ps. 126:6).

He will laugh!

# 13

# MOUNT
# MORIAH

*"God will provide for Himself the lamb."*
*—Genesis 22:8*

BREAKING THE SILENCE that follows a great movie, my husband often remarks, "There is only one story." The theme plays out in countless ways, but the heart of the plot remains unchanged—a hero lays down his or her life to save another. We cannot help being moved. Even atheists love the Christ-figure. But Your story, Father, is harder to find in our tales. It is not that You have hidden Yourself, nor that we lack a strong archetype. It is just that Your story is too awful for us to stomach, and thus we look away.

I have a Jewish friend who wrestles with his faith. He has been zealous at times, unbelieving at others. He does not understand my fascination with Abraham. "Abraham was a terrible father," he tells me. "If God were to tell me to sacrifice my son, you know what I would say! Let Him kill me. That is evil!"

We may be reticent to admit it, but most of us wrestle with the story of Abraham's test. For years I hated thinking about it. I could not square the binding of Isaac with Your goodness, Father. I could not imagine why You, Who are love, would ask such a terrible thing of Your servant. How could You put Abraham through such agony, even knowing You would spare his son? Did You not know Abraham's heart already? Surely You were not jealous of the son You had promised. I could

126

not believe that. Nor did I think did You would test Your friend needlessly. But why? What purpose did it serve in Your plan?

Your command seemed to play straight into the Accuser's hand. With each reading of the story, I could hear Satan whisper in my head— "Is this God of yours really good? How can you know what is good if He required Abraham to act contrary to His own law?"

Then the Accuser would turn his venom on me. "You know you are not able to do what Abraham did. God tests all His people with dreadful trials. He will test you, and you will fail."

I shuddered at the sound of that voice. I hated the doubts it left in its wake. I resisted by singing the psalms or reading the parables— focusing on the comforting parts of Scripture. It was a decent defense. It quelled the voice of the enemy for a while. But I could not forget the charge entirely. A nagging fear remained lodged in the back of my heart.

Now I understand that I was looking through the wrong end of the telescope! The binding of Isaac is not a tale of what You demand from men; it is all about what You give! It is the gut-wrenching tale of a father who, in love, offers that which is dearer than his own life for the sake of another. The story is hard for us humans to swallow because we have not yet experienced complete union with another. We cannot offer another without violating that other's will. But so perfect is the union within the Trinity that such offering is possible. The distinction of God's Persons makes the offering more terrible and costly than we can imagine, but it is not a violation of will. We need a model to help us grasp such love. We need a window into Your heart, Father.

This is why You orchestrated a prophetic event, unique in human history. You enacted a drama conveying Your plan to save us. And when You surveyed the world for someone to play Your part, Your eye fell upon Abraham.

What love You must have held for Your servant! What faith You placed in Your friend! How beautifully You wrote the test on Mount Moriah to foretell the cosmic drama played out at Calvary. And how richly You have rewarded our father for his faith!

The Genesis account begins with these words:

> Now it came to pass after these things that God tested Abraham, and said to him, "Abraham!"
>
> And he said, "Here I am."

> Then He said, "Take now your
> son, your only son Isaac, whom
> you love, and go to the land of
> Moriah, and offer him there as a
> burnt offering on one of the
> mountains of which I shall tell
> you."
>
> —Gen. 22:1–2

Father, the words You used to name Isaac are words that also describe Your Only Begotten. Jesus is Your Son, Your only Son, the One whom You love. He is the only Person like You, the only One who knows You fully and can fully return Your love.

I imagine, Father, that the Incarnation cost You far more than we can comprehend. Though Jesus was never lost to Your sight, You were lost to His vision and to His memory. Your Son became an infant with all the vulnerabilities of humanity—pain, hunger, fear, and loneliness. He depended upon Mary and Joseph to protect Him. You also relied upon Mary and Joseph to train Your Son as the Holy Spirit guided Him, enlightening His mind and revealing You to Him. You watched as Jesus grew and came to understand His identity. You delighted in Your Son on the day of His baptism, but You restrained Yourself when the enemy came to tempt Him. You trusted Jesus, in the frailty of his flesh, to choose obedience.

Living in time and in a mortal body, Your Son experienced desires that warred against Your will. You allowed the unity of the Trinity to be tested in ways that astounded the angels. The choice was real, I believe. You would not intervene. There can be no love where there is no freedom. But You knew the choice had already been made in heaven. You trusted the Son as He trusted You.

For Abraham, Isaac's birth was pure joy. It was a joy heightened by years of waiting. A joy made complete by the fulfillment of Your word. The bond Abraham felt with Isaac grew in a type of triune wonder shared with You and Sarah, for he knew that Your plan was the reason for their joy. Isaac, for his part, understood that he was a promised child with a prophetic destiny. He realized that his father's identity as a prophet was proven in his very existence.

I wonder what Your voice sounded like the day You summoned Abraham to Mount Moriah. You had spoken to Abraham many times when he had not responded so swiftly. Abraham had proven he was not afraid to engage You. He had questioned Your promise and laughed in Your presence. He had interceded with boldness for Lot. But this time he did not protest. He simply summoned Isaac and left.

Did He know You better now? Or was there a quality to Your voice that was somehow different this time? It must have been dreadful and holy, but not without hope, as the writer of Hebrews suggests. Perhaps Abraham heard in Your call an echo of Your own dreadful fiat—the pledge made within the Godhead before time began, each Person of the Trinity committing His role in the salvation of mankind to the Others. "Let it be done unto Me according to Our word."

> So Abraham took the wood of the burnt offering and laid it on Isaac his son; and he took the fire in his hand, and a knife, and the two of them went together. But Isaac spoke to Abraham his father and said, "My father!"
>
> And he said, "Here I am, my son."
>
> Then he said, "Look, the fire and the wood, but where is the lamb for a burnt offering?"
>
> And Abraham said, "My son, God will provide for Himself the lamb for a burnt offering." So the two of them went together.
>
> —Gen. 22:6-8

A father, a son, and a flame ascended Mount Moriah—three actors in one drama.

Surely the Holy Spirit burned in Abraham's heart, giving him strength, inspiring the utterance of salvation's mystery, "God will provide for Himself the Lamb."

The Spirit must have burned within Isaac as well, enabling him to climb the mountain laden with wood, much like Jesus ascended Calvary under the weight of His cross. The Spirit enabled Isaac to trust his father, standing still as Abraham tied ropes around his arms and legs. Isaac could have fought back. According to rabbinic tradition, Isaac was in the prime of life, like Jesus at the time of His crucifixion. Isaac could have overcome his elderly father. Jesus could have called angelic hosts to slay His enemies. But they both chose a different path. They chose to drink the cup their fathers set before them.

It was imperative that trust between Abraham and Isaac be preserved in this test, for You would be Isaac's God as well as Abraham's. If Isaac were to doubt Your goodness or resent the obedience of his father, how could he father a nation for Your Name? When You spoke from heaven to stay Abraham's hand, Isaac must have felt Your jealous love for him. He heard Your voice with his own ears, as his father had heard You in the past. Isaac heard Your voice as Jesus heard You at His baptism. And when he heard Your voice, Isaac came to know his father in a new way. He came to know himself as well. The truth he had heard from others was written on his heart in that moment. He knew that everything You had promised to Abraham was promised to him. His was the seed that would be blessed and multiplied! His was the family that would become a great nation. His was the bloodline through which all the nations of the world would be blessed. The sound of Your voice and the knowledge of Your pleasure was more than compensation for his fear. He had heard the living God and lived! Isaac returned home with his father in peace.

It was even more imperative that Your unity with Your Son be preserved in the Passion, for if Jesus should resist Your will, more than our salvation would be lost. The unthinkable would happen—the love that created the universe would be disrupted at its source. Father, this is a mystery beyond my sight. I know that You hold all things in Your hand and that Your union with Your Son cannot be shaken. But I think that Satan tried. It was his tactic against Your Son's humanity, both in the wilderness and at the crucifixion, to question His identity. "If You are the Son of God, . . ." he taunted, "then prove it to Yourself. Turn stones into bread. Throw Yourself from the Temple. Come down from the cross." At the Passion, the enemy unleashed the forces of hell upon Your Son— heaping mockery upon beatings, humiliation upon betrayal, thirst upon agony. His goal, I believe, was not primarily Jesus's death. He knew that You, the Author of Life, held authority over death. Satan had seen You raise dead men before. His deeper desire, I think, was for Your Son to resist Your will, to question Your goodness, to exert rage in the extremity of human suffering. Satan wanted Jesus to call the angels down from heaven and abort the plan. That would have been true victory for him—discord between Father and Son.

You could not intervene at the cross as You did for Abraham, for Your Son was the Lamb You provided for the world. This test would have to run its course. The blood of Isaac had no power to save, for he was a sinner like all of us. Taking his life as a mere test would have been evil, I think. But Your Son was different. You were one with Him. The blood that ran through His veins carried life eternal, and His death could confer that life to sinners. His sacrifice would make visible Your love in a way that no other gift could. His submission would usher us humans into the fellowship of the Trinity. For this prize, You sent Him to die, and You suffered in silence, trusting the Spirit to strengthen His heart.

What unspeakable love You must have felt for Your Son as He surrendered His spirit to You! Holy grief and pride and triumph running together. What honor and glory You prepared as His reward! You have placed all authority in heaven and on earth into His hand! At His name, "every knee should bow, in heaven and on earth and under the earth, and every tongue acknowledge that Jesus Christ is Lord" (Phil. 2:10–11 NIV). And this will be to Your glory and vindication, Father, for it was Your will from the beginning to exalt Your Son.

You have remembered Abraham, too, for his offering moved You deeply. His act of faith was a necessary participation in Your plan of salvation, preparing us to understand the price of the gift You gave. You established a lasting memorial at the site Abraham named "the Lord provides." You chose Mount Moriah as the dwelling place for Your Name. You instructed David to have Solomon build the temple there (see 2 Chron. 3:1), and there You came in glory to dwell with Abraham's children. On that mountain You received their offerings and You forgave their sins. No wonder David called this mountain "the joy of the whole earth" (Ps. 48:2).

135

You invited foreigners to Your temple as well. Gentiles like myself found joy in Your house of prayer. Magi from the East traveled there to inquire about the star heralding the birth of the Savior. This is why Jesus felt such fury when He found robbers in Your house. He knew His Father to be the Provider, not one who steals from men.

More than any man, Jesus understood Your role in salvation. We Christians tend to think primarily, almost exclusively, of Jesus when we think of salvation, but Jesus always gave You credit. He was, and is, eager to glorify You just as You delight in exalting Him. Jesus made it clear from the beginning of His ministry that Your love was the driving force of salvation. In the most famous summation of salvation in Scripture, He told Nicodemus, "For God so loved the world that He gave His only begotten Son, that whoever believes in Him should not perish but have everlasting life" (John 3:16). Jesus emphasized Your sacrifice rather than His own.

As the time of His crucifixion drew nearer, Jesus spoke more often about His love for You, and Yours for Him. "I will do what the Father requires of me, so that the world will know that I love the Father" (John 14:31 NLT). "The reason my Father loves me is that I lay down my life—only to take it up again" (John 10:17 NIV).

Jesus's words concerning His passion help me understand that it was His love for You, more than His love for us, that motivated Him. Jesus loved You unto death, and because of this I know Your love for us is without measure. You would not sacrifice the Son who loved You so dearly if the prize for His suffering was not a worthy reward.

Oh Father, I'm sorry that I ever doubted Your goodness! I am sorry that I was blind to Your suffering in the salvation story! I imagined You to be jealous and cruel when, in truth, You were giving Your heart to men! I feared Your motives when You called Abraham to offer his son. Now, however, I am undone at the thought that You draw men into Your own story. Those who know You best, You will allow to share in Your suffering, and that is a gift of intimacy.

I love my Jewish brothers and sisters who embrace the story of Abraham's test without the resolution I see in Jesus. I know their faith moves You, just as Abraham's did. You could not explain Your reasons to Abraham, for that would have cut short his freedom. You do not reveal Your plans or Your symbols before their appointed times. Yet Abraham and his offspring have chosen to believe in Your goodness, and that belief is an act of friendship.

Abraham, if you can hear me in heaven, I thank you for your belief, for your example, for your love for Isaac and your love for God! I am grateful to you for playing the Father's role in a redemption story so awful it has been enacted only once.

And, Father, I stand in awe of Your unfathomable gift! Thank You for giving Your children of the dust more than we could possibly ask or imagine. Your words to Abraham have become my confession of praise to You: "Now I know that You love me, Lord, for You have not spared Your Son, Your only Son, for me."

# 14

# A BRIDE FOR ISAAC

*Isaac . . . took Rebekah and she became his wife, and he loved her.*
*—Genesis 24:67*

I FIND IT INTERESTING, FATHER, that Abraham and Sarah seemed in no hurry for Isaac to marry. I would have thought otherwise, given their age. Before I reached fifty, I was ready for grandchildren. I wanted to see my fun-loving son playing with kids of his own. I looked forward to watching my daughter's belly expand with life. And my hope was rewarded. My two eldest children now are parents. I love gathering the young ones in my arms, singing over them, blessing them, commending them to Your care. How much more, it seems, would Sarah and Abraham long to see the spreading of Isaac's vine, for the hope of Your promise lay in his fruitfulness.

But no. Their hearts were full, it seems. Their doubts were quelled, their joy complete. They were content in their love for one another, satisfied to live as a family of three under Your watchful care. They remind me a bit of the holy family, tucked away in Nazareth, sharing a divine secret with one another. Perhaps in some distant, imperfect way, they served as a sign of the love among the Persons of the Trinity.

But Abraham, Sarah, and Isaac were mere humans, prone to jealousy and fear. I get the impression that Sarah was none too eager to share her boy with another woman. Perhaps it was best for all concerned that she was never tested as a mother-in-law. No effort was made to find a bride for Isaac until Sarah had passed.

Some rabbinic traditions suggest that news of Isaac's binding precipitated Sarah's death. Some say the horror of the report sent her into shock. Others say it led to a separation between Abraham and Sarah, which is why Sarah died in Hebron, though Abraham went on to Beersheba after the test on Mount Moriah. This is just conjecture, of course. I hold to the hope that the grace that allowed Isaac to submit to his ropes moved Sarah to faith as well. Lord, there are many things You have chosen to veil from our eyes, countless secrets known to You alone. Whatever may have transpired in this chosen family, I know they were ever close to Your heart. I know their joy is now more perfect, whole, and united than it was during their sojourn on earth.

Sarah was 127 years old when she died, which made Isaac thirty-seven at the time. Abraham wept and mourned at her death. He also faced a practical problem. He wanted to honor his wife with a proper resting place, but he was a sojourner in the land.

I find it very much like You, Father, that the only property Abraham owned in his

lifetime was a tomb. The land in which he
wandered never belonged to him. He
purchased the cave of Machpelah in Hebron as
a burial place for Sarah. The cave became his
earthly resting place as well. That is where
Isaac and Ishmael came together in peace to
bury their father. It is where Isaac and
Rebekah were buried. It is where Jacob asked
his sons to take his bones when they left the
land of Egypt. The bodies of Abraham, Isaac,
and Jacob all rest in the one spot Abraham
owned waiting on the fullness of the promise.

It was not until Sarah died that Abraham's
thoughts turned to a bride for Isaac. Suddenly
the urgency of planning for Isaac's future
seemed to dawn on him. The days of the
happy threesome were gone. Isaac was in
mourning. Abraham was old. The time had
come to look forward, to act in faith according
to the promise.

> So Abraham said to the oldest
> servant of his house, who ruled
> over all that he had, "Please, put
> your hand under my thigh, and I
> will make you swear by the Lord,
> the God of heaven and the God of
> the earth, that you will not take a
> wife for my son from the
> daughters of the Canaanites,
> among whom I dwell; but you

shall go to my country and to my family, and take a wife for my son Isaac."

And the servant said to him, "Perhaps the woman will not be willing to follow me to this land. Must I take your son back to the land from which you came?"

But Abraham said to him, "Beware that you do not take my son back there. The Lord God of heaven, who took me from my father's house and from the land of my family, and who spoke to me and swore to me, saying, 'To your descendants I give this land,' He will send His angel before you, and you shall take a wife for my son from there. And if the woman is not willing to follow you, then you will be released from this oath; only do not take my son back there." So the servant put his hand under the thigh of Abraham his master, and swore to him concerning this matter.

–Gen. 24:2–9

Indeed, an angel did precede Abraham's servant. And when he arrived in Abraham's homeland, Your Spirit inspired this prayer:

> "O Lord God of my master Abraham, please grant me success today and show steadfast love to my master Abraham. I am standing here by the spring of water, and the daughters of the townspeople are coming out to draw water. Let the girl to whom I shall say, 'Please offer your jar that I may drink,' and who shall say, 'Drink, and I will water your camels'—let her be the one whom you have appointed for your servant Isaac. By this I shall know that you have shown steadfast love to my master."

> —Gen. 24:12–14, NRSV

The sign Abraham's servant sought became an enduring pattern for romance in Scripture. A man meets a young woman at a well and asks her to draw water. She responds humbly, with kindness. The man's heart is won, and he asks for her hand in marriage. This is how Abraham's servant found Rebekah. It is how Jacob fell in love with Rachel. It is how Moses met Zipporah. And similarly, it is how Jesus

approached a woman living in the shadows of
Samaria.

The signs of the patriarchs show us the
romance that inspired the Incarnation! This is
a truth I hardly dare to believe. Father, You
were willing to send Your Son so that He
would have a Bride. You wanted His joy to be
complete! You loved Him more than Abraham
loved Isaac, and You knew Your Son longed
for a Bride. You desired His life to bear much
fruit so that You might see His image in many
sons and daughters. So Abraham's promise
was enfolded into Your desire for Your Son.
"For this reason a man shall leave his father
and mother and be joined to his wife, and the
two shall become one flesh," Paul writes,
quoting Genesis. But then he goes on, "This is
a great mystery, but I speak concerning Christ
and the church" (Eph. 5:31–32).

Jesus told us plainly that He was a
bridegroom, but we missed Him. We continue
to miss Him, I think, by taking His parables
too figuratively. We fail to see the twinkle in
His eyes when He tells stories of a king who
invites his citizens to a wedding feast in honor
of his son. We don't get the irony, the mirth,
the divine tenderness at play. Jesus, the
storyteller, is acting as the messenger in His
own parable. He is the prince in disguise. He
comes at the behest of the king, inviting his

own citizens to the banquet. The invitees fail to recognize the messenger as the son. They are too engaged in their own affairs to clear their calendar for the king. They are not, however, too busy to beat the king's servant and kill him. No wonder the king is furious! (See Matt 22:1–14.)

When the noblemen and landowners refuse their summons, invitations are sent further—to the least of the king's citizens, to resident aliens, to outcasts like the Samaritan woman. Those never invited to a banquet before are more willing to come, and what a surprise they receive! The lowly messenger who invited them turns out to be the prince! What is more shocking—they themselves are the bride! The banquet is for them! They have been invited to join the royal family and given embroidered robes. No wonder the guests who refuse their wedding garments are cast out. The prince's bride must not appear at her wedding in rags. Isaac's bride certainly did not.

> Then [Abraham's] servant brought out jewelry of silver, jewelry of gold, and clothing, and gave them to Rebekah. He also gave precious things to her brother and to her mother. . . .
>
> So they sent away Rebekah their sister and her nurse, and

> Abraham's servant and his men.
> And they blessed Rebekah and
> said to her:
>
> "Our sister, may you become
> The mother of thousands of ten
> thousands;
> And may your descendants possess
> The gates of those who hate
> them."
>
> Then Rebekah and her maids
> arose, and they rode on the camels
> and followed the man.
>
> —Gen. 24:53, 59-61

Father, I love to think of Israel, and the church, and myself, as Rebekah on a journey to meet our Lord. Your servant, the Holy Spirit, tells us stories about our Bridegroom—stories of His kindness, His wealth, His power. As we travel, the Spirit teaches us what pleases our Husband. He adorns us with jewels—good works prepared for our hands. We come to know about Him. We come to trust His heart. Through the Holy Spirit, we are even able to hear His voice. But we have not yet beheld His face.

I find the account of Isaac and Rebekah's first meeting profoundly beautiful, both as a human love story and as a prophetic picture.

Now Isaac came from the way of Beer Lahai Roi, for he dwelt in the South. And Isaac went out to meditate in the field in the evening; and he lifted his eyes and looked, and there, the camels were coming. Then Rebekah lifted her eyes, and when she saw Isaac she dismounted from her camel; for she had said to the servant, "Who is this man walking in the field to meet us?"

The servant said, "It is my master." So she took a veil and covered herself.

And the servant told Isaac all the things that he had done. Then Isaac brought her into his mother Sarah's tent; and he took Rebekah and she became his wife, and he loved her. So Isaac was comforted after his mother's death.

—Gen. 24:62–67

Isaac was alone when he met his bride. He had gone out to the field to meditate, as Jesus often left the crowds to seek You, Father, in solitude. Isaac was staying in the desert, at Beer Lahai Roi, where Hagar named You the God Who Sees. Isaac knew Your mercy just as

Hagar did. You spoke from heaven to spare them both. But Isaac knew there was a reason for the mercy that stayed Abraham's hand. His life held a purpose that could only be fulfilled in marriage.

When Rebekah saw the lonely figure, she asked Abraham's servant who he might be. Upon learning it was Isaac, she got down off her camel and veiled herself. She did homage to the one who would be her husband.

Jesus, I cannot wait for the day when I meet You face-to-face! I long to see You in the fullness of Your glory, surrounded by the host of heaven singing Your praise. But first I hope to meet You alone, as Rebekah met Isaac, or as the Samaritan woman found You at the well. I want to come dressed in the gifts of the Holy Spirit. I want to bow low at Your feet. And though this sounds too bold for human desire, I hope to see in Your eyes that my love brings You some measure of joy, some comfort or vindication for Your suffering—both on the cross and in union with Your people.

I am touched by the fact that Isaac brought Rebekah into his mother's tent. Sarah was the first woman he had loved. She was the woman who had given him life and nurtured him. She was the one who had taught Isaac all he knew about feminine love; but she was gone, and he missed her. Scripture tells us that Isaac kept

Sarah's tent and her belongings close to himself. Isaac opened his heart to Rebekah by bringing her into the space reserved for his mother; but Rebekah would expand his heart, loving him in ways that Sarah could not.

I wonder, Father, if there is not some parallel here with your own Son? Israel, Mary, and the church are all mothers of the Messiah, each in her unique way. Israel carried the seed that led to His birth and was entrusted with the Law and the Prophets that prepared His way. Mary gave birth to Your Son in the flesh and instructed Him in the ways of Your people. The church has borne witness to Jesus throughout the world, giving birth to many souls. In this way she is also a mother of the Messiah. Jesus said that all who do His will are His mother (see Mark 3:33–34). And yet, our relationship will change.

Mothers welcome sons into their world. They nourish, nurture, and teach their boys within their own homes. Brides, on the other hand, go to live in their husband's house. Abraham would not permit Isaac to return to Haran. Neither will You, Father, allow Jesus to live on this earth again, at least not in its current state. Rather, You call the Bride to the New Jerusalem where we will eat at His table and walk in His ways. Someday all of us, Jews and Gentiles, "will come from east and west, and sit down with Abraham, Isaac, and Jacob in the kingdom of heaven" (Matt. 8:11). We will finally see Your Son face-to-face. Then "we shall be like Him, for we shall see Him as He is" (1 John 3:2), and the transformation will make us fit to live with Him.

On that day, when faith becomes sight, the mission of both Israel and the church will be accomplished—not forgotten but fulfilled. The earth as we have known it will change. The old will pass away. A new reality will dawn in which Your people, both Jew and Gentile, are transformed into one Bride for Your Son.

No one's uniqueness will be lost. Our stories from earth will never grow dim. Rather, each one's history will be seen in the full vibrancy of its color, the full weight of its import. Our stories are inseparable from Your Son's story. To lose any of their particularities would diminish His glory. The names of Abraham's great-grandsons will be inscribed on the foundations of the New Jerusalem. The names of the apostles will mark its gates. Sarah, Rebekah, Ruth, and Mary will always be honored as mothers. Abraham will forever be Yeshua's father, just as he will be mine.

Soon Your Son will ride forth from heaven as a Bridegroom in all His glory. The cave of Machpelah will open and the patriarchs will ascend. All their children, numerous as the stars, will rise with them. We will be seated at the Marriage Supper in our wedding garments, waiting for the Bridegroom to appear. When He does, we will fall on our faces and bow at the feet of our Lord. On that day His joy will be complete and all will laugh together in wonder.

# ABOUT AMY COGDELL

Amy Cogdell lives in Elgin, Texas, with her husband Thomas and two of their five children. She and Thomas serve alongside others in the leadership of Christ the Reconciler, a lay community of Catholics and Protestants praying and working for reconciliation within the Body of Christ. She spends her days homeschooling, praying, writing, and keeping house. She serves as the chair or co-chair of two boards of directors—Christ the Reconciler and Antioch Network. Her other book is Unity Through Repentance: The Journey to Wittenberg 2017 (co-authored with her husband Thomas, published by William Carey Publishing, in 2022).

www.christthereconciler.org/history

# SHH!

Amy's husband Thomas here. Shhh! Don't let her know I've hacked into her book! I'm her biggest fan, so I want to especially thank you for taking the time to read her first full book, *In the Bosom of Abraham*. If you are interested in bonus material available only to the readers of this book, use the super cool QR code I've created below, or visit the link

<u>https://bit.ly/abraham-xtras.</u>

<u>T</u>his will take you to a special, hidden website. There, you can see some artwork of Abraham's life that Amy likes.

Clicking the QR also lets you:

- find out about another amazing book that Amy is working on,
- subscribe to her blog,
- sign up for our personal newsletter that we use to keep friends up to date on our comings and goings, and
- even contact her to let her know what the book meant to you.

Thanks for your interest!

And remember, mum's the word! Don't let her know I did this. (She really doesn't like QR codes!)

CAN YOU HELP?

*Reviews are everything to an author because they mean a book is given more visibility. If you enjoyed this book, please review it on your favorite book review sites and tell your friends about it.*

*Thank you!*

Made in the USA
Coppell, TX
02 June 2024

33047295R00102